Chaos and order in the world of the psyche

[handwritten dedication: For Margaret — with best wishes for all her chaos confrontations, present & future. May they be fruitful! Joanne]

Chaos can enter our lives in many different ways – through death, divorce, conflict with family, friends, or at work. Joanne Wieland-Burston, through her work as a Jungian analyst, is no stranger to chaos, and frequently acts as companion, support and guide to those whose lives are in turmoil.

She shows that the experience of chaos is generally both negative and frightening, destabilizing the individual and provoking feelings of insecurity. People, therefore, often seek to deny and avoid chaos – but chaos that is blocked off does not disappear. It manifests itself in depression, fear, anxiety, and various physical symptoms, often making us incapable of performing the simplest daily tasks. The author describes how she helps people to learn to meet the chaos, to accept and see it in a different way – as the starting-point for a new order in their lives. This 'organic order' is better suited to their needs and personality, and provides them with the basis to come through their chaos and to lead fuller, happier and more satisfying lives.

Joanne Wieland-Burston explores the modern attitude to chaos, showing how we shun and deny it whilst at the same time overestimating the importance of orderliness. Contemporary western society has no tools to deal with chaos, unlike 'primitive' cultures whose myths, tales and rites reveal a deep commitment to developing and transmitting to future generations models of chaos confrontation. Wieland-Burston draws upon these ancient cultures and upon modern scientific findings of chaos theory to show how we can regain the wisdom that we once possessed and have now lost.

Joanne Wieland-Burston is a Jungian analyst and psychotherapist in private practice.

Chaos and order in the world of the psyche

Joanne Wieland-Burston

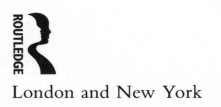

London and New York

First published as *Chaotische Gefühle* by
Kreuz Verlag AG, Zürich © 1989

First published 1992
by Routledge
11 New Fetter Lane, London EC4P 4EE

Simultaneously published in the USA and Canada
by Routledge
a division of Routledge, Chapman and Hall, Inc.
29 West 35th Street, New York, NY 10001

© 1989, 1992 Joanne Wieland-Burston, Breitsohl Literarische Agentur,
Zürich

Typeset in 10/12pt Bembo by
Falcon Typographic Art Ltd, Fife, Scotland
Printed and bound in Great Britain by
Biddles Ltd, Guildford and King's Lynn

British Library Cataloguing in Publication Data
A catalogue record for this book is
available from the British Library

Library of Congress Cataloguing in Publication Data
Wieland-Burston, Joanne.
  Chaos and order in the world of the psyche /
Joanne Wieland-Burston.
  p. cm.
  Includes bibliographical references.
  1. Life change events. 2. Adjustment (Psychology).
  3. Chaotic behavior in systems – Psychological aspects.
  4. Order – Psychological aspects. I. Title.
  RC455.4.L53W54   1992
  155.2'4 – dc20   91–40117 CIP

ISBN 0–415–07212–3
     0–415–07213–1 (pbk)

Contents

Illustrations

Introduction

'I don't know what's the matter with me – everything's upside down; the whole world seems chaotic.'

Chaos is the starting point for most psychotherapies. Its impact is such that one feels stunned, helpless. In the face of such turmoil one turns for help, professional help. The psychotherapist becomes the companion, the support and the guide in the encounter with chaos.

Of course, what chaos is for each individual varies. For some, it is the separation from a loved one, be it through death, divorce, or even leaving home. For others, chaos is caused by conflict with the surrounding world – with family, friends, the boss, colleagues. And for still others, inner conflict triggers chaos – conflict between seemingly irreconcilable feelings, needs, impulses, ideals. Often chaos appears primarily in the form of a frightening symptom – depression, fear, palpitations, trembling; it comes up out of nowhere and makes one incapable of performing the simplest daily tasks.

That which evokes the experience of chaos knows innumerable personal variations. But, generally speaking, all chaos experiences share a few basic traits. They are negative and frightening and they destabilize the individuals, provoking in them distinct feelings of insecurity. It is, thus, completely understandable that people try to avoid chaos. But this avoidance in itself just makes things much worse.

Chaos which is blocked off does not disappear. It merely remains unknowable and guards its deep dread. In the course of therapy we learn to meet it, to accept it, to differentiate it. Ultimately, chaos can be seen in a different light. It appears as the starting point for a search – the search for a new order. And, as we invariably discover, it was not chaos, but the inflexibility of the prevailing order which created the difficulties in the first place.

Our contemporary world is marked by a definite 'anti-chaosity'. At the same time, we are, most of us, engaged in an unconscious search for chaos. We are inhabited by a secret lust for chaos which we attempt to satisfy in many ways.

Other cultures have devoted more conscious energy to chaos. Their myths, tales, and rites reveal a deep commitment to developing and transmitting models of chaos confrontation to future generations. It is just such wisdom that is lacking among us. As chaos is disdained, avoided, and rejected, we find ourselves without the necessary tools for dealing with it.

During the course of psychotherapy this lack must be remedied. We need to develop ways and means with which individuals can meet their chaos. The examples of these other cultures provide us with valuable hints on how we can do so.

Another main concern is finding a more personal sense of order that is better suited to the individual and his life. Evidently the ordering system of the past was intolerant. It rejected new material, stamping it as chaotic. But this material is part of the personality; it cannot be rejected without serious damage to the integrity of this personality.

The type of order we are seeking is personal and flexible. It shows a high degree of chaos tolerance. 'Organic order', as natural science's most recent investigations define it, corresponds well to our needs. This order characterizes living systems: capable of adaptation to ever-changing conditions, such systems can go through periods of chaotic instability on their way to finding new and more appropriate forms of order.

Our personal order may well be grounded in our bodies. That would help explain why physical symptoms often play such an important role in chaos experiences. The physical 'disorder' would actually be the initial sign of a necessary transition phase, prompting us to seek a new order that is better suited to our actual life situation.

The essential importance of chaos within such a context is immediately apparent. Chaos is a dynamic aspect of all living systems. Without it, organisms would stagnate, or even cease to exist. In this context, suicide and death appear as the end result for systems that cannot integrate chaos. Their incapacity to be led through chaos into new order means death. As in nature, the psyche that cannot traverse chaos is doomed to stagnation and lifelessness.

Investigating the importance of chaos within the psyche helps us to re-examine its place in our world. Such a re-evaluation cannot take place too soon. Our inimical relationship to chaos hinders our growth and adaptation to the ever-changing needs of our lives. Peace research is only naive idealism if it is not complemented by conflict research.

A preliminary chapter serves to introduce the problem which will occupy the centre of our interest throughout: the threat we sense in chaos and our search for security in order. First we shall define our terms in their linguistic context, taking into consideration the realm of common life experiences. As the history of the two words reveals, for the Ancients of Greece and Rome chaos and order were both quite neutral, even potentially positive terms. In the formlessness of the 'chaotic abyss' they saw the *prima materia* of the world. 'Order' derived as it is from the art of weaving, readily became identified with mythological conceptions of divine predestination.

In stark contrast are our contemporary evaluations: for us chaos evokes not the creation of the world but rather its destruction. Order takes on contrasting hues of security and even, at times, radiates a certain aura of holiness and sacredness otherwise so foreign to our age.

But this is only the conscious side of the question. Everyday life experiences attest to the fascination which chaos can and does exert on us. Its formlessness can be the invitation to experiment and discover the unknown; in this context of meaning, order becomes the equivalent of constraint and the compulsion to conform. It takes on the inimical role formerly ascribed to chaos. Revolutionary movements of all kinds – on the political but also on the social scene – subscribe to such evaluations. But even the most respected and well-established members of society have always integrated a certain well-measured degree of chaos in their daily lives. Whether they flee the boredom of too well-organized social forms in adventurous explorations of the depths of Africa, in colonialistic ventures, or even in jet-set tourism to exotic corners of the world, all sought and seek a bit of the unexpected, the unpredictable, the formlessness that is the essence of the realm of chaos.

Our conscious denial of the value of chaos is seriously detrimental to us. Rejecting it a priori, we are relatively helpless when it strikes, be it in the form of an automobile accident or a psychic crisis. Faced with chaos in crashes (of the stock market or of transport vehicles), in accidents (at nuclear energy plants, etc.), or in clashes between and within human beings, we are quite surprised, stunned, and find ourselves unable to react in an adequate manner. Chaos has no place in our culture's particular image of the world, despite the fact – so clearly evident in the preceding examples – that it is an integral aspect of life. As we shall see in Chapter 2, our so-called 'primitive' forefathers seem to have been well aware of chaos's place in the universe. They reckoned with it and spent substantial amounts of energy on finding ways and means of meeting it. Vestiges of the practices and beliefs with which pre-scientific cultures met chaos (when it struck in natural catastrophes, sickness, sterility, death, war, mishaps and anomalies, and in new and different situations of all kinds) have come down to us in popular belief (superstition) and in contemporary rituals (both sacred and profane).

Fairy tales, myths, and religious rites tell the story of these ancient ways of dealing with chaos. In this material from the collective unconscious we can discern two major patterns of chaos encounter: the one, the masculine/confrontational, the other, the feminine/accepting. Whereas the first examines and distinguishes the component elements of chaos, the second accepts and appreciates the potential value inherent in it.

Psychotherapy makes use of a combination of both modes, as we find in certain still extant aquatic initiation rites. Whenever people are 'driven to desperation' (Eliade 1977) by a chaotic event and consult a psychotherapist, the ensuing chaos encounter follows this type of combination model. The emotional acceptance of chaos and its potential value is the indispensable basis for an active and conscious confrontation with it.

When, however, as is often the case, we are not in possession of appropriate models for such an encounter, we spontaneously tend to avoid chaos. Chapter 3 is devoted to portraying the fate of three individuals who reacted in such a helpless way. We shall present here the cases of two heroines from the world of fiction (and their real, human counterparts) and of one real young man whose withdrawal from chaos and concomitant erection of fortresses of order are both typical and tragic. The order which rules in Odintsov's well-run but emotionally empty life (in Turgenev's *Fathers and Sons*) leads her to depressive phases and a loveless life. Edith's make-believe world of peace and order (in Patricia Highsmith's *Edith's Diary*) protects her from the tumult of disappointment only to precipitate her untimely death. And the compulsive attempts to control all of what normally belongs to life actually seem to trigger a young man's psychotic episode. All of the compensatory ordering efforts are intended to help re-establish a much needed sense of security. They are characterized by their exaggeration, their rigidity, and their claim to exclusivity. For a certain time, at least, they do protect people from chaos, but they also cut them off from the flow of life. And, paradoxically, a chaotic crisis often ensues. That is what happens in all of our three examples: depression, mental illness, and death occur. In real life we may find slightly more nuanced reactions to extreme adherence to order. Some of them are less shocking than our examples. But all reveal the fact that the person has come to a dead-end. When we are unable to find appropriate new ways of dealing with modified conditions in our lives – when change seems impossible – we fall into stasis. We hold on to our antiquated order, which subsequently becomes our prison. On the one hand, we feel safe, for nothing new or unpredictable can reach us. On the other hand, our developmental capacities are severely impaired: our freedom of movement and of choice are restricted.

Natural organisms which cannot adapt to changes in their surroundings and remain fixed in an unsuitable order tend to die out. This fact has led biologists to stress the importance of sensitivity and flexibility in the fight for survival. An organism must be able to sense alterations in conditions as they arise and to adapt accordingly. Chapter 4 surveys scientific discoveries on the nature of chaos and the role it plays in the flux and flow of natural processes.

Science has ascertained that chaos is not necessarily an end but can mark the beginning of a new order. Furthermore, certain ordering phenomena can be observed within chaos itself. We shall outline the pertinent scientific information in ten points and proceed from there to examine their eventual applicability to human life.

As will become apparent, the most vital traits for our development are, as in nature, sensitivity and flexibility. In psychotherapy, the encouragement of their development is a major goal.

Chaos encounter and the search for organic order in psychotherapy – that is the subject of the final chapter. On the one hand, we follow the models discussed in Chapter 2 and, on the other, those suggested by the scientific phenomena described in Chapter 4. The search for organic order can be conceived of in human terms as retrieving the natural flexibility of the point of view. As our examples from Chapter 3 demonstrated, the order evolved as a defence against chaos is severely restricted and restricting. A person's image of himself and the world becomes too narrow to embrace the diverse elements of his experience. Withdrawal takes place. Re-establishing the capacity for direct contact with present experience leads to the expansion and differentiation of the point of view and, simultaneously, to the enlargement of the personality.

Case studies will show how we proceed, first to encounter the initial chaos and then go on to take up the search for the organic order which uniquely suits each individual. We pay special attention to psychic material as it presents in images and the imagination – both of day- and night-time – and to the body's specific reactions. This procedure, however, is not feasible or desirable for all who seek psychotherapy. Some people most urgently need to retrieve a certain sense of security in their former order, however unsuited the latter may actually be to their own personality and situation.

A final example serves to show the rather rarer cases in therapy of those who do not seek a therapist because of a chaotic life experience. Their long successfully repressed chaos is often coupled with an unconscious fear of order and a striking lack of points of view which they can call their own. The therapeutic situation is especially difficult for them, for reasons which we shall point out. However, the long-term goals here differ in no way from those of the majority of cases discussed. We attempt to help individuals develop their sensitivity for chaos and their capacity for dealing with it, all the while seeking the specific, individual order which corresponds to the particular persons and their needs.

It seems as though we are entering into a new era in our relationship to chaos. More and more people are getting involved in some sort of psychotherapeutic work in an attempt to meet their chaos. Science is reasserting the importance of chaos in our world. And, as a result, other fields of investigation have begun to delve into the question of chaos. In the past few years many books and articles have been devoted to the topic.

The question which arises is the extent to which this new chaos-inclusive image of the world will affect the men and women of the future. Will the children of tomorrow, brought up with the knowledge and conviction of the necessity of flux and flow in life, be less susceptible to the fear of total chaos and to the seduction of immutable order? Might their intimate acquaintance with the great ordering machine – the computer – also favourably influence their attitude to chaos and order? Will their confidence in the computer's capacity for ordering and revealing order in the most chaotic data grant them more confidence in the face of chaos? Although a world picture definitely forms and influences those in whom it is engrained, it is doubtful that the problem of chaos and order can be resolved in this way. For behind the archetypal threat of chaos and the compensatory search for order lie fear and insecurity. And they will continue to be the lot of humanity even in the twenty-first century.

Order always seems to offer us security. Its importance for us cannot be denied. But the core challenge of the human condition is resisting its hegemony. Every time we fall victim to the illusory promises of peace and harmony in order and reject and neglect chaos we are trying to escape the reality of life and the insecurity which necessarily belongs to it. The results are invariably catastrophic. Adhering to an exclusive, compensatory order destroys the capacity for development, rendering both the individual and the society unfree. It has led, in the past, to humanely unacceptable situations – from war to the extermination of entire groups of people. And it threatens to continue to do so.

Our dire need is to find a more communicative relationship with chaos, to accept and examine it, to include it in our image of ourselves and of the world. This is a process which we must engage in on the level of the individual first of all. For, as long as we cannot become more open to our own, personal divergences, we cannot become more open and tolerant of the divergences which pervade the world around us. Delving into the many facets which make up our own psychic individuality helps us to resist the temptation of homogeneous self-images. And in the long run, it is this direct experience of our own multi-dimensionality which will make us able to accept and deal with that of the world outside. C.G. Jung stressed the way in which getting to know oneself helps bring the individual into communion with the world at large. This communion, this openness for communication, is the basic prerequisite for our finding new and more adequate solutions in the face of chaos in the life of the individual and of the society.

Chapter 1

Chaos and order in our world

Most contemporary Western societies are marked by a definite denigration – if not to say quite simply, fear – of chaos. Denying the validity of chaos as an aspect of experience goes hand in hand with the exaggerated value we tend to place on order.

But these evaluations do not belong to the essence of chaos, as linguistic analysis alone attests. The etymological roots of the word and its mythological background indicate that chaos was once associated with creativity. This association has been recalled by numerous innovative movements in the past. Today, too, certain individuals and groups share such views. Most of us, however, consciously reject and retreat from chaos while unconsciously seeking it. In fact, our world is marked by the prevalence of a relatively unconscious lust for chaos which knows many forms (from games to gambling, to adventure journeys and wild partying); it clearly compensates for our conscious denigration of chaos and concomitant over-valuation of order.

In this preliminary chapter the elements of chaos will be examined: its denotations and connotations. I shall then turn to etymology and mythology, which offer quite a different picture. The ambiguities belonging to chaos will become most evident in the way we actually experience it today. Here we find the other side of the coin. In the various manifestations of the cultivation of chaos as it is practised in contemporary society and as it was practised in the past, we can discern the attraction chaos exerts on humanity.

I shall then delve into the world of order and try to discover the underlying causes for its idealization among us. Reference to earlier cultures especially reveals a certain basis for our emotional reliance on order. And, in this context, I shall broach the major question that will occupy our interest in the remaining chapters: how can we find adequate means of encountering chaos without having to reject it entirely in favour of the illusory promises of order.

A mere passing glance at the pages of our dictionaries gives us a good idea of the way things stand. Chaos is granted relatively few lines of explanation while a lengthy commentary is devoted to order. Order evidently has a wealth of associations; commonly used, it forms part of our basic vocabulary. One could say that in this sense it is like bread, a staple food belonging to our daily diet. The concept of order is a basic concept, a staple word, belonging to our daily vocabulary. Can we go so far as to say that knowledge of the word 'order' is indispensable to communication? Such is certainly not the case for chaos. One can well imagine speaking English, French, German without even knowing the word. We use it rarely. Chaos appears rather as an exotic food, not necessary to life, not important for existence. Does the paucity of associations – compared to order's wealth – really mean that chaos is not so important for us? Or is it rather like a denizen of another realm that we keep at arm's length for fear of its encroaching within the boundaries of culture?

Defining this unwelcome creature is apparently a simple matter. It signifies confusion of any kind: disarray, jumble, clutter, snarl, muddle, even lawlessness and anarchy (*Webster's*). Duden's *Dictionary of Synonyms* mentions confusion and anarchy while the *Random House Dictionary* stresses the utter confusion and disorder of chaos and the *Brockhaus Encyclopaedia* limits itself to the idea of confusion in general. Less simple is the explanation of the negative overtones we hear in the word. There is a definite sense of destruction in the definition of chaos as anarchy. And '*Chaote*', a German neologism, sounds the same note. The term '*Chaoten*' was first employed in the 1960s to describe the 'members of a political group that strive to accomplish their goals through the violent destruction of the established order'. '*Chaote*' is further extended to designate a person who 'continually causes disorder and confusion' (Brockhaus).

And so we see how the word chaos has grown to encompass not only a lack of order – a neutral condition in itself – but also the destruction of a given order. From the purely verbal opposite of 'system' and 'cosmos', chaos has become 'opposition' to the system, 'destruction of the cosmos'. The aggressive implications are clear and the fear which chaos therefore arouses in us begins to make sense.

The demonization of chaos we observe here – the aggression as well as the destructiveness – does not belong to the original meaning of the word, as we shall see. It is the result of a specific attitude to order – one of idealization. Only if we identify order with positive, even ideal, traits, can its lack be judged so negatively. Chaos would be the mere negation of order, were it not for the fact that we over-estimate the value of order itself.

This becomes apparent as soon as we approach order and its myriad meanings. Order has so many different meanings and is used in so many set phrases (the *Oxford English Dictionary* (1989) devotes six pages to 'order'), that it is actually quite difficult to define. We may say that it is associated with regularity, norms, discipline, and moral rectitude. Order also implies meaning, for all ordering is accomplished according to a predetermined core of significance.

The universal use of the catch phrase 'OK' testifies to the ubiquitous importance of order in contemporary life. 'OK' stems from the old English phrase '*oll korrekt*'; it is most often adopted into other languages in its original form, but is sometimes translated. All of the translations have to do with order: French, '*en ordre*': German, '*in Ordnung*': Hebrew, '*be sedar*'. The world over, people say that things are 'in order' when they are right, all right, well, good, as usual, when they correspond to our image of how they should be. Order is the touchstone of the civilized world, the world of culture, cultivation and 'anti-chaos'. And, in fact, our linguistic usage of the term shows the extent to which we identify with the principle of order. 'Law and order' are the basis for our political and social systems. Whenever this basis is endangered, those within the system voice the cry for 'law and order'. And so they call upon the 'forces of order'. The latter have been trained to protect the system against whatever might be endangering it at the moment: unusual weather conditions, criminality, political agitators. Accidental occurrences of any kind – those that are not pre-planned as part of the normal order of things – are matters of concern for the forces of order. They are there to help bring things back into order (rule, discipline, regularity), so that all may as quickly as possible once again conform to our expectations.

The world of order is apparently the exact opposite of the world of chaos. Here the predictable and dependable, 'normal' course of things; there the unpredictable, undependable, and abnormal is the rule. Here we can enjoy the calm reassurance of expectations being fulfilled, there we sense the jolting irregularity that threatens our sense of well-being.

Let us now take the plunge into the realm of chaos, to discover how we really experience it in daily life. We tend to use the word most frequently when speaking of unusual traffic conditions. When a sudden or unforeseen snowfall hits a city and drivers, caught unawares, lose control over their automobiles, 'chaos' often ensues. Cars go slipping and sliding over the thoroughfares without the slightest regard for the customary law and order of the streets.

Normally, intricate rules and regulations carefully channel the progress of vehicles along our city streets. The reigning order is extremely complex, but we hardly realize it for it has become second nature to us. To get an idea of what traffic can be like without such regulations, we need only read the newspaper reports of those early years of the automobile. Life must have been truly terrifying: there was even talk of having to resort to lynch law in order to punish careless drivers!

And so, in our day and age, it is only when something abnormal occurs – an unusual storm, a drunken driver, a washed out bridge – that we can imagine what such lawlessness can feel like. Our conventional order is wiped out; the accidental gains the upper hand. Despite our perfectly designed laws, cars speed off in unpredictable directions, countering all attempts to keep them on their prescribed course. A state of complete confusion, usually involving the destruction of material and human lives, takes over. Chaos reigns.

Faced with the unpredictability of an automobile rushing at us on the wrong side of the street, zigzagging at a horrendous speed, we can duly feel endangered by chaos. In view of the damage that must ensue, the destructiveness we sense in chaos is absolutely justified. Yes, in such circumstances, chaos is frightening, terrifying. It clearly poses a threat to us. But let us pause now in our visions of horror and dread. Let us meander over to the lazy joys of an amusement park. What do we see here?

Children, but not children alone – teenagers and also some adults – are careening into each other in miniature cars, laughing and screaming as their dodgem cars twist and turn. And in the background, the music of a popular song. What we understandably felt to be so frightening and threatening on the streets, we somehow find amusing, cause for diversion here. The unpredictable, chaotic situation takes on a completely different feeling tone in the context of the amusement park.

Of course, there is nothing really perilous about the dodgem car situation. It is a game. We pretend that we are in danger, but then manage quite well to get out of the jam and go off to avenge ourselves on the driver who just bumped into us. We play with the fantasy of risk and enjoy meeting the 'accidental', reacting quickly, going off undaunted to new collisions. In our miniature cars, in this privileged space, we can live out all the emotions that would belong to chaos were it not really so frightening, so potentially destructive.

Before leaving the amusement park with its preview of chaos lust (which will be investigated further later on), let us dwell for a moment on real-life dodgem car drivers, that is, those people who take a secret joy in reckless driving on the roads. Well aware of the danger to which they are exposing themselves, it is just this danger that stimulates the excitement they experience. But it is indeed a secret joy. One rarely feels prepared to admit to it. Only in an intimate moment and not without a sense of guilt, can one express the sense of excitement, the thrill of the sweet and forbidden fruit that this irrational behaviour offers. We are in the other world now, that of chaos lust, lust for the chaotic which finds so little room within the confines of our too well ordered universe. This initial example provides our first inkling of another side to chaos. It is a realm holding not only terrors; it can also be exciting, amusing, fun.

An experiment with a group of educated adults confirms this observation and adds other facets to our image of chaos. The group was asked to give their spontaneous reactions to the words 'chaos' and 'order'. The results appear in Table 1.1. At first chaos was judged in a definitely negative way: fears arose immediately. People said they felt overwhelmed and insecure in the face of chaos; whereas, in relation to order there was an unequivocal sense of comfort and security, an impression of being in control. But, suddenly, the tables turned. As soon as order was associated with compulsion, then chaos could be seen in a positive light. New aspects of its experience came to mind: the excitement of new possibilities, openness to surprise and creativity, the potential for development. These traits gained the upper hand. Once the element of fear retreated into the background, chaos became the domain of creative experimentation. Chaos and creativity is a theme for reflection. For other cultures the combination has sounded less foreign. Even the etymology of chaos points to the possibility of such a connection. Chaos stems from the Greek '*khaos*' which means 'gaping emptiness', an innocuous enough term that does not immediately evoke ideas of creativity. The 'gaping emptiness', linguistically related to a 'gaping abyss' ('*khasmas*'), has come down to us in the words 'chasm' and '*khasmas*', a medical term for a pathological condition: excessive yawning. This modern derivative is explained by the fact that the verb '*chainein*' (to which '*khaos*' is related) means 'to gape' or 'to yawn'.

Of paramount interest for us is the history of the Greek usage of '*khaos*'. It was used to describe the original state of the world,

Table 1.1

Chaos	*Order*
Fear	Comfort
Dejected	Liberating
Incomprehensible	Comprehensible
Senseless	Meaningful
Unsettling	Calming
Insecurity	Security
Overwhelming	Conquer, manage
	Confidence
	Overall view, perspective
Question	Answer
Provocative	Control
	Economical
	Factual
	System
	Meaning
Disharmony	Harmony
	Habit
	Compulsion
	Fear
Relaxed	Tense
Exciting (pleasant excitement)	
Development	
Possibilities	
Surprise	
Creativity	
Liveliness	
Fantasy	

before it was ordered into a universe. The *prima materia* of the world, that is, chaos. Now the reasoning begins to make sense. The 'formless void' was the state from which the process of creation was undertaken by the demiurge.

Actually, creativity does have to do with a formless original state upon which we act. The lack of form may at first glance seem frightening; it is, however, the lump of clay from which something new can be formed. But this formlessness of chaos is exactly the point upon which individuals differ. For some, it is too threatening: the void of the abyss must be filled, the disordered brought to order and made to fit into known forms and categories as soon as possible. It must be made to conform to some known order. For others, it is the ultimate in excitement, as it opens up space for an original and imaginative encounter with the raw material. Making our way back to present-day experience of chaos, this lack of forms, this gaping abyss that constitutes the roots of chaos helps us to understand what takes place in a chaotic moment. Let us call to mind such a moment.

The forces of nature create a situation which we cannot spontaneously master. We are hit unprepared, for example, when ice covers the city streets or a shortage of water makes itself felt. We are quite helpless; our habitual patterns of behaviour are insufficient to meet the situation adequately. Our conventional rules of conduct, our normal ways of behaving leave us resourceless. We do not immediately know how to handle the unexpected turn of events. But, suffering together with others under the freak conditions can lead to new combinations for action and interaction, in other words, to creative solutions.

In this connection, the example of Chile comes to mind. Suffering together under a repressive government, in economic distress as well, the women of Santiago organized street kitchens where thousands were fed daily. As the women were unemployed, they had time to take care of the kitchens. Having little to eat, the people pooled whatever they had. The lack of work and food could not be met by any known patterns of behaviour. There is no set way of dealing with such difficult conditions. Some new and unhabitual way of reacting had to be found. The creative solution of installing soup kitchens filled the void. It is no less than the creation of a newly ordered world that was accomplished by the women of Santiago.

Examples of quite opposite reactions to chaos are not difficult to come by. Think of what happens when a traffic accident occurs.

The scene often becomes one of gaping. Spectators stand around those injured; they stand and watch, gaping. As if paralysed, they look on, both fascinated and helpless. Lacking in pre-set behaviour patterns for the situation, not knowing ways to respond to what they see before them – remember, chaos is formless – they are helpless. And so, they await the arrival of the 'forces of order' who come to take chaos in hand. The latter have been trained to cope with chaos, in all its multifarious forms.

Of course, another psychological motivation for the passive spectator is his fascination with chaos. Our daily lives are so well-ordered, everything has become so regulated, following its predetermined and expected course, that we have developed a definite need for something accidental, something which does not meet with our expectations. Invariably, the majority of the curious on-lookers are people whose lives are otherwise dominated by a quite compulsive attention to order.

So, we see that chaos can evoke very different reactions. Spontaneously, most of us tend to react negatively. The more we are personally attached to order, the more it means to us in our lives, the more difficulty we experience in reacting spontaneously to its sudden and unexpected disappearance. We are 'hit', rather than stimulated by it: we become its victims. But the more inner distance we have from rigid order, the freer are our interactions with chaos as we meet up with it in the world within and around us.

Getting involved in the accidental combinations of chaos, letting oneself be taken up in the flow of events and seeing what happens can be experienced as exciting. Art and creativity require such a playful attitude. In allowing oneself to be led on by the unexpected, the accidental, one makes room for the discovery of new, previously unsuspected images and ideas. New combinations appear before us. Uncontrolled by our conscious will, they find juxtapositions that can be unusual and even inventive.

Yes, chaos can be a field for experimentation, its openness an invitation to go beyond fixed, conventional boundaries to complex, playful patterns. New possibilities of vision, of action and interaction can arise from chaotic juxtapositions. The component elements, set free from predetermined conceptions of the way things must be, can find their own order.

Such considerations immediately bring to mind the endeavours of artists and other creatively-minded individuals. Within the field of art (but also of politics), there have been periods of great enthusiasm for the conscious cultivation of chaos. Of all of the periods of Western art, above all the movements known as Dada and, in its wake, surrealism, have sung the praises of chaos. The artists – painters and poets – of this era based their faith on chaos and its potential for revitalizing an art that had become stultified in dusty, convential forms of the past.

Recalling the endeavours of the artists of that period, we recognize in their words and works the high esteem in which they held the characteristics of chaos that we have discerned: the senselessness, the destructiveness, the openness to new possibilities, the capacity to unsettle and to provoke alike.

To get a precise idea of what Dada and surrealism (and their direct foreruners, the Italian futurists) stood for, we might take a look at two ready-made objects by Marcel Duchamp. Duchamp was not an official member of the surrealist group but he participated actively in the movement. His first 'ready-made' he called *Bicycle Wheel* (1913). It consisted of a bicycle wheel mounted on a block. Three years later he submitted a French pissoir to an exhibition of the Society of Independent Artists only to have it refused. He consequently withdrew from the Society. These objects were obviously not meant to conform to any preconceptions of what art is supposed to be about; they are more like a manifesto, a statement of position saying something like: 'Art is whatever takes one's fancy. It needn't be beautiful. It needn't meet up to anyone's expectations.' This non-conformist attitude characterizes Duchamp himself especially well. In time, he retired completely from the field of 'art' and spent the rest of his life playing chess.

What the surrealists valued above all was the imagination. Their pleasure lay in the oneiric atmosphere created by the illogical juxtaposition of words and images they pursued in their works, but also in experiments with the unconscious. They practised what they called automatic writing – letting words flow with as little conscious intervention as possible. They were fascinated by dreams and visions and were avid supporters of the new science of psychoanalysis.

But, as is basic to any and all of the chaos-oriented movements, the surrealists were adamantly 'anti': anti-art, anti-clerical, anti-establishment. Whatever values were cherished by the establishment, the surrealists adamantly rejected. Their rejection of ruling values led them to consider themselves as revolutionaries.

Some of them even joined the communist party, but eventually withdrew because it was not revolutionary enough.

The conscious cultivation of chaos has naturally been supported by more strictly political movements, like the Russian anarchists or even the German Red Brigade. Destroying existing systems of order to make room for new and different systems has always been the preoccupation of the political agitators, whether they are called *chaoten* or anarchists, terrorists or agitators.

Whether their intent is renewing art forms or political systems, those who glorify chaos all see in it liberation from predetermined conceptions. Either traditional art or established government is felt to be standing in the way of the innovators. Their sense of the negativity of the order of their day makes them its enemies. For them the existing order makes them unfree, ties them in cords of bondage, prevents them from expressing themselves and developing in the manner that suits them.

In this respect, one must add to the inventory of collective chaos–cultivators the movements of young people. All youth movements, in all times, have always been more or less chaos-oriented. From the battle of the new gods against the old, from the *Sturm und Drang* movement to the beatniks or Hell's Angels, the Punks and the New Wave generation, all have attempted to disturb and unsettle, or at least to shock the generation of their elders. Granted, the degree to which they were consciously bent on aggression and even destruction of the established order varied greatly. The basic, underlying tendencies of all of these movements, however, is identical. And it must be so. For youth movements, as manifestations of the archetypal conflict between the generations, testify to the inherent need of each new generation to assert itself. Each must find its own means of expression, its own forms, ideals, and approach to life. From this perspective, the order and conventions of 'the fathers' are more or less inimical to any and all free development. And to a certain extent this is true: the expectations the young sense coming from their parents can stand in the way of their becoming themselves.

Chaos cultivation has to do with freedom and independence, with liberating oneself from pre–set forms and expectations. And it is in this sense that we can comprehend the quite unconscious lust for chaos prevalent among us. It denotes a search for a space in which things do not happen according to the pre-dictions. It means getting involved in unforeseeable circumstances in which anything could potentially happen. It helps to stimulate the sense of excitement that we feel in an unknown situation.

Our lives are otherwise so well organized, everything has become so reliable and predictable that most of life's commodities can be taken for granted. We need not reckon with the possibility of the unexpected. We can generally count on our images of the future being fulfilled. We can rely on the world of order that we have built up around ourselves.

But order without chaos is a truly lifeless matter. Without the prospect of the unexpected, the accidental, the disordered, our lives would be so stable as to be unbearable. We would stagnate in the arms of bureaucratic boredom.

We need to experience chaos and what it stands for. But this need is mostly unconscious. Few would go to the extremes of declaring their lust for chaos. Few would associate with the aims and ideals of anarchists or *chaotes*. Most of us have neither the desire to destroy nor even really to shock our fellow citizens. But most of us feel and live out the need for something outside the bounds of our daily order.

This need for a field of experimentation in which we can feel the challenge of meeting the unforeseeable lies behind a great many of the amusements, games, and entertainments of our too well ordered universe. These needs can be lived out in more or less extreme forms. At the far end of the scale lie adventure journeys; the safaris of yesterday, undertaken with guides and gear, have recently been up-dated to offer still more excitement. The crossing of the Sahara on motorbikes, the Camel Trophy through wild territories, survival vacations in the wilderness, all provide the opportunity to satisfy our modern yearning for chaos. But much tamer versions of the same thing also exist. Games of chance – from cards to lotto – permit the common citizen to enter into contact with the ticklish risks of the accidental and unpredictable within dimensions that are bearable for him. And, one must not forget the pleasures of the consumer world. On the one hand, they confirm our need to fit into an established order: we must go along with the fashion of the day. On the other hand, they always simultaneously appeal to our need to feel different, original, special. Not only the normal, standardized order, but also the wild, new, and different style entice us to buy.

But if this is so, if a deep lust for chaos dominates us all so, why this secrecy? Why is our search for chaos not consciously cultivated, as it was by the surrealists or by the anarchists? Or, to speak quite simply, why can we not openly admit to the pleasure we take in reckless driving?

Chaos lust is unconscious because we consciously cling to order. We value the order of our society, the order of our lives, in such an exclusive manner that the unconscious opposite takes over. The phenomenon is called compensation. It simply means that that which we consciously value has its opposite in our unconscious. The more one-sided this conscious attitude, the more extreme the unconscious opposite becomes.

As we shall see on the individual level in Chapter 3, 'Individuals in the face of chaos', the greater the threat of chaos, the more we stress the importance of order. We hold up order before our eyes like a protective shield whenever we feel the approach of chaos. We observe the same phenomenon on the level of the collective. This certainly has a basis in our psychological constitution. For, as we shall see, we have a special relationship to order that stems from our human capacity for consciousness. Another reason for our collective exaggeration of the value of order is related to the fact that our order is a sham. In the face of the chaotic threat of nuclear war that hangs over us, we cling to the facade of the good order of things, for it helps us to repress this terrifying eventuality. It provides us with an illusion of security.

There follows, now, an investigation of the nature of order and the security and comfort it seems to offer us. We want to try to understand why order elicits such feelings in us, and to work at uncovering the mechanisms which make chaos and order such bitter foes. These mechansims have to do with the essence of order itself.

Let us first refresh our memories as to the qualities assigned to order. We saw from our dictionary definitions that discipline, regularity, and norms are associated with order, that it has to do with meaningfulness and system. Consequently, the emotional reactions elicited are security, comfort, ease, liberation (freedom), confidence, and a sense of perspective (clarity). The underlying principle that elicits such feelings is actually control. When things are in order, when we can order them, we have the impression that we have them in control, under control.

But control is a double-edged sword. If it is enforced by a strict system of order, then we are faced with compulsion. Gone are the impressions of freedom and ease. Being compelled to comply to a system of order can make us feel tense and nervous, afraid. Order can then be as threatening as chaos was. Once again, the reactions depend on the individual.

As chaos's linguistic derivation helped us to discover hidden layers of meaning, let us also examine order's past history. Order derives from the Latin word '*ordo*'. A *terminus technicus* from the art of weaving, it describes the ordering of the threads in the woof. Like chaos, order has an ancient mythological history which can be traced through images of weaving.

In the mythology of many peoples, weaving is related to the fate of the world. It is like giving birth; the weaving loom refers to the structure and movement of the universe (for Islam, for example). Plato uses weaving as a symbol of the world. The goddesses who spin and weave the fate of men are a repeated mythological *typos*. In the Roman context from which our word stems it was the *Parcae* or the Fates who spun, measured, and cut the thread of the lives of men and women.

Already in this ancient world of association the relationship between order and security, but also between order and compulsion, was an established fact of life. We know that the Romans considered even the chief of the gods himself (Jupiter) as relatively powerless in the face of the Fates. When the three fatal sisters decided that a man's thread was to be cut, then cut it must be. No being, human or divine could interfere with the ultimate decision of the Fates. Their power was a central element in the belief in predestination. Fate was pre-planned, pre-decided; only service to the gods could influence Providence. There was no margin for disobedience: the power of the divine order was unshakeable. It was a compelling reality and had to be respected as such.

The security which such a system offers can be understood as a kind of holding. We can best imagine it in the words of the Negro spiritual song 'He's Got the Whole World in His Hands'. The image radiates the security, ease, and comfort of being supported and held in the arms of a parental figure. The confidence in the deity is basic: He is naturally felt to be strong, loving, and concerned about one's welfare. And obviously, His power, the order He established, is not to be questioned.

Figure 1.1 shows a fifteenth-century sculpture which well illustrates the kind of holding the religious world of that time offered. Linked with the belief in the divine right of kings, the Church

Figure 1.1   'Schutzmantelmadonna' (Madonna of the Cape)
Source: reproduced by courtesy of Dr Helmut Hell, Kunstwissen-
schaftliche Photographie, Reutlingen

provided a framework of meaning and order which granted to each and every creature on God's earth his allotted place. For individuals, such an ordering meant that each had their own rung on the ladder of being. It also gave them a set pattern to follow. Everyone knew how they were expected to act, what they were to do and not to do in order to conform to the God-given order. Duties and rights, expectations and privileges were clearly defined. There was no room either for doubt or for non-compliance.

The obligation to comply with the system's rules was enforced. Not only were trespasses severely judged in the afterworld. During life on earth, too, punishment for disobedience to such a sacral order was harsh. Trials were held and burnings, excommunications, and other severe penalties could be pronounced for relatively harmless trespasses. Because it was of divine origin, this order demanded complete submission.

We are immediately reminded of our most recent example of such a system. The government of the Ayatollah Khomeini in Iran bore obvious resemblances to the religious state described above. In Iran, too, crimes were punished severely, as crimes against God and the divine order. A religious meaning was assigned to war, so that death in battle took on a positive significance for the individual and his family. Even participating in a holy war lent a whole new dimension of meaning to life and death. And this framework of meaning 'held' its believers. But it tolerated no deviations.

Although order has undergone severe modifications in our world, that which it promises appears immutably anchored in the human soul. We no longer live within the kind of cosmic ordering system that people of the past knew. Most of us do not depend on the support of a church or a deity to stand by us in time of need or set out for us our duties and privileges. And, with the virtual disappearance of this pillar of support in the other world has also come a considerable diminishment of the compulsion to conform: we are subject to relatively few legal restrictions on our social behaviour. But, at the same time, a certain framework of meaning is gone.

And yet, when we ask ourselves what we spontaneously associate with order, the words security, meaningfulness, and control come up. Order, order itself, carries these meanings for us. The era of the god figures is over or ending, but order retains its divine characteristics.

In fact, when we refer back to our dictionary definitions, we can see that order is described today in the same terms which earlier peoples used to define their gods and heroes. Order stands for moral rectitude, discipline, regularity. Order is divinized or at least idealized. It has become a value unto itself. This fact explains a great many interesting, but otherwise unfathomable dilemmas of our world. It helps us to understand how it is possible for human beings to perform atrocious crimes in the name of order, to follow inhumane orders with a servile fidelity.

When we consider that in the place of a divinity, order itself reigns, then the holiness of ordering systems for some individuals can be interpreted as a form of religion. Once one reasons within such an ideology, then the seriousness of order and the demonization of anything which might disturb it becomes comprehensible. Order offers security and meaning; if some thing or some one endangers it, our illusions are threatened. Harmonious meaningfulness and the sense of control can no longer be maintained in the face of disruptions. These must be rejected, demonized, in some way depotentiated.

Often the cause of the disorder is sought in the outside world. It is projected there on whatever does not fit into the system – frequently outsiders, inimical elements, foreign elements, be it people – one's neighbours, one's wife – or even one's own body. Once the cause of chaos is pinned down there, it can be fought there and the illusions of inner harmony and control within the ordering system can be maintained.

Of major importance here is the avoidance of chaos. It must not be allowed to encroach within the system. Thus we can understand the extreme emotionality of the question of order. How often do we witness the heated discussions among neighbours concerning the order that is supposed to reign in the apartment building? Compliance to the regulations is a serious matter. Similarly, within one family the discussions on order and how it is kept, or rather not kept, are not uncommon. They can attain a degree of importance and intensity that surprises us, and yet, they continue to preoccupy us and dominate our relationships in a strange and compelling manner.

In caring for order we are doing no less than creating a world, structuring it and making it coincide with a certain predetermined image. We are making it conform to our expectations of dependability and stability. The importance of these values is not be under-estimated. Such considerations belong to the essence of our being human. We need to feel that we can depend on our environment. We need to be able to count on its stability, on its basic and unswerving reliability. Naturally, this is not always one hundred per cent so, and cannot be so. But the general, underlying need accompanies us from the cradle to the grave.

Ordering is one aspect of this dependability. We are beings which order and which need order. We perceive the world and classify our perceptions according to ordering schemes. This process has to do with our human constitution. We are gifted with consciousness, a capacity which makes us able to become aware of ourselves and the world. And consciousness functions according to various processes of ordering. In this way we perceive, differentiate, and digest our perceptions, learn and, hence, develop. Ordering is a basic trait of consciousness. Without it we would constantly be overwhelmed by the information of our senses. Not being able to apperceive, we would be submerged by the diverse bits of perceptions that flow into our organs of perception from all sides. We would be able neither to sort out our experiences nor to learn to respond to them.

Order helps us to orient ourselves in the world. Without this orientation we would be completely impotent. Simple proof of this phenomenon is found in the plight of prisoners in solitary confinement. Deprived of reference points according to which they can orient themselves, in time they lose the ability to walk straight. Without order and the possibility of orientation, we become unable to perform the simplest of tasks.

We definitely need order to be able to exist and function in the world. Our problem today, however, is that we have become too exclusively fixated on order. This fixation serves the pretence of assuring ourselves that we have everything under control. We consciously avoid any encounters with chaos and hold tight to our illusions of order and harmony. In this way we cannot learn to deal with chaos adequately. We cannot learn to differentiate its elements and eventually to integrate them into other systems of order. Our capacity for growth and adaptation is, therefore, stunted.

We have forgotten the age-old traditions for dealing with chaos. For they do exist. Passed down from generation to generation in folk tale, myth, religion, and ritual, patterns and models for the encounter with chaos provided the people of the past with a certain sense of security in which we are lacking. Most adults living in contemporary society have never been exposed to patterns of dealing with chaos. They have never had the opportunity of observing how their parents or their grandparents dealt with chaos. Instead, the pretence of order and harmony dominates our images of the world. Chaos and its conscious experience are avoided. This is the root of our desperate clinging to order, and of modern humanity's helplessness and panic in the face of chaos.

Chapter 2

Collective patterns of chaos encounter

In our common human heritage known as the 'collective un-conscious' we discover the patterns of chaos encounter that are so sadly lacking among us today. Handed down from generation to generation, this material shows us how our ancient ancestors regarded chaos and how and when they attempted to deal with it. In the present chapter the basic patterns for encounters with chaos that are found in fairy tales, myths, religious belief, ritual, and superstition will be described. The material under discussion will also help us to deepen our understanding of the nature of chaos itself.

Chaos was a threat for our early ancestors as well as for us. Primitive peoples are renowned for their fear of the unknown. And when does the unknown manifest more clearly than when one is faced with a new and unusual situation? No custom, no habit, no previous experience provides comforting reassurance of the outcome. One cannot foresee how things will develop, whether they will turn out well or badly. Thus, all beginnings, all first encounters are potentially dangerous and can evoke deep anxieties. This attitude is well illustrated in the popular saying 'The first step is the hardest'.

In order to deal with the new and unpredictable which belong to the essence of life, early societies developed rituals and told stories. They were duly repeated at times of beginning, whenever a new year, a new season, a new phase in life, a new situation loomed on the horizon. They were meant to guarantee safe passage through these periods, from the old, accustomed order of affairs to the new, as yet unknown, and therefore unpredictable and frightening order of things. Between the old and the new order lies the upheaval of chaos.

The pertinence of this material for psychotherapy becomes apparent when we recall the fact that chaos is the starting point for most psychotherapies. Generally, the chaotic moment marks a new phase in life. It appears chaotic because it is new; so we meet it with feelings of fear and mistrust and defend ourselves against it. But, as long as chaos remains rejected and hence undifferentiated, we are at a dead-end. Only when we can find means of dealing with it adequately, can we learn to encounter it as our 'primitive forefathers' did.

In the wealth of material belonging to the collective unconscious we can discern two basic patterns of chaos encounter. I call them the masculine/confrontational and the feminine/accepting. In the former, a heroic figure meets a representative of chaos – or a chaotic situation – face to face. A battle or a showdown ensues. The hero manages – with the help of his special powers – to disband, destroy, or depotentiate chaos. In the latter, a less obviously heroic, even an anti-heroic figure (or attitude) prevails. He also meets chaos, but in a rather passive manner: he allows himself to be touched or moved by it, accepting it or in some way appreciating or integrating it. A third type of pattern – a combination of these two – exists. It is still practised among us today in religious rituals – in the Jewish mikvah and the Christian baptism. This model corresponds the most aptly to the psychotherapeutic chaos encounter. We shall examine it at the end of the chapter.

The most impressively monumental descriptions of the masculine mode of chaos confrontation are to be found in creation myths. One specific type of cosmogony shows how a divinity creates the world by a process of differentiation, consciously dividing a chaotic *prima materia* into separate parts. This image underlies the identification of chaos with creation which we pointed out in Chapter 1.

The Babylonian creation myth, the *Enuma Elish*, is a fine example. It bears striking resemblances to our Old Testament account of the beginnings of the world. But similar examples exist in Vedic literature. Although we are mainly interested in the way Marduk, the hero and supreme god of the Babylonian pantheon, vanquishes his chaotic opponent, Tiamat, we shall first have a look at the events preceding the battle. Only then can we appreciate the immensity and significance of Marduk's feat.

In the beginning there is nothing but water, the water of the primal parents, Apsu and Tiamat, and their counsellor, Mummu. They mingle together in a formless whole. No differentiation has taken place as yet; the myth describes this state in the following terms:

When above the heaven had not (yet) been named
(And), below the earth had not yet been called by name
(Tablet I, ll. 1–2, in Heidel 1974)

That is, the elements of the world had not yet been distinguished from each other, for naming is a way of distinguishing.

What we have here is the total pre-conscious unity of the primal state. The waters of the unconscious reign (water always symbolizes the unconscious). No hand of consciousness has reached in to separate the elements from each other. This is the 'formless void' which we have come to know as chaos.

Slowly, a process of differentiation begins: children and then grandchildren are born to Apsu and Tiamat. They have names, distinctive traits and are described as gods, with special, superior qualities, for example

Lahmu and Lahamu came into being; they were called
    by (their) names.
Even before they had grown up (and) become tall,
Anshar and Kishar were created; they surpassed them
    (in stature).
(Tablet I, ll. 10–12, in Heidel 1974)

The growth in consciousness that these developments represent is a threat to the old, unconscious state, Apsu. He protests that the gods make too much noise and prevent him from sleeping and, determined to put an end to the disturbance of his peaceful unconsciousness, he devises (with Mummu's help) a plan to get rid of his children. Tiamat their mother, pleads for leniency but is overruled. Were it not for Ea, one of the grandchildren, the gods would have been destroyed and the world would never have been created. But Ea discovers the plan and kills Apsu.

Tiamat decides to avenge her husband's murder and, for this purpose, devises a whole army of monsters. She is so horrible-looking thus equipped for war that none of the gods have the courage to meet her face to face. Here Marduk steps in. Grandson of Ea, he promises to fight Tiamat if the gods pledge to name him their supreme chief. Marduk is consecrated in a grand ceremony after which he proceeds to arm himself for battle and ventures forth to meet Tiamat.

As we saw, Tiamat is the mother of the gods. Her name has been understood to mean 'chaos'. She stands for the formless primal waters as a whole (symbolically, for the unconscious) and is often represented as a dragon. But this *massa confusa* is the *prima materia* of the world. It requires merely the hand of a creator to perform the transformative ordering of its substance.

Figure 2.1 shows Marduk with Tiamat at his feet, she the water and dragon, he the solar king and hero. His regal traits are indicated in the decorative robe, the jewellery, the ring, and the staff. His solar qualities (symbolizing the light of consciousness) are seen in the rosette decoration (sun symbols), the staff (an instrument of differentiation which points and guides), and the feather head–dress (symbolizing the birds, and the upper regions of being, i.e. the intellect). Representing the light of consciousness as he does, Marduk is the ideal opponent for Tiamat, the representative of the darkness of the undifferentiated unconscious. The way in which he confronts her clearly confirms this. He looks, examines, reflects, and decides, applying his intellectual powers to the task of dissecting the formless

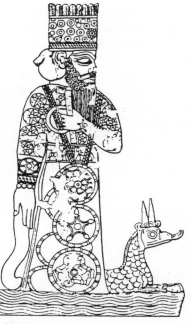

Figure 2.1   Marduk
Source: Heidel (1974)

mass of Tiamat. After he has once vanquished her in battle with his mighty instruments, he rests, 'examining' chaos. He reflects on how best to proceed, for he wants 'To divide the abortion [and] create ingenious things [therewith]' (Tablet IV, 1.136, in Heidel 1974).

What follows is a monumental, mythic feat of ordering. Marduk distinguishes and separates elements of the *massa confusa*. First, he divides the body in two, and partitions off the sky:

He split her open like a mussel into two (parts);
Half of her he set in place and formed the sky (therewith)
    as a roof.

(Tablet IV ll. 137–8, in Heidel 1974)

He proceeds in like fashion to examine and measure the regions, making the earth, Esharra, as counterpart to the sky, then dwelling places for the gods and for the stars 'their likenesses'. He creates not only space, but also time, determining its passage by defining its divisions. In appointing Nannar the moon god to light up and take care of the night, he separates day from night and thus brings forth the cycle of night and day. Finally, having fashioned Lullu (mankind) to serve the gods, and Babylon, Marduk establishes Esagil, the temple of the gods, in Babylon. This is the final act of creation in the Babylonian cosmogony.

Our Old Testament account follows this same model, although it points to a further level of development. Here, too, the initial state of the world is the undivided waters. All is covered in darkness: one can see, distinguish, recognize nothing: there is no cognizance, no consciousness as yet. The Hebrew original text uses the word '*tohuwabohu*' to describe this state; the word means chaos or confusion. Then God steps in to confront chaos, dividing light from darkness, creating the heavens. He, too, like Marduk, collects the waters in one spot so that dry land can appear. And, he goes on to create light by making two astral bodies.

The parallels to Marduk's actions are astounding. Also, further on in the Genesis text, God divides and distinguishes as Marduk does. What characterizes our God-image is that He 'speaks' where Marduk 'determines'. The gift of language indicates a further step in the evolution of the human race.

This type of creation myth is well illustrated by William Blake's The Ancient of Days (Figure 2.2). Here we see a divine figure reaching down over a formless void, measuring and dividing it up with the tools of consciousness – here, a compass. The creation of the world results from this primal ordering of chaos.

This model of chaos encounter is typified by the confrontation of an undistinguished, unconscious mass by the powers of conciousness. The ordering which is then performed brings light to darkness, brings forth solid earth where shifting waters used to

Figure 2.2   William Blake, The Ancient of Days (1794), Whitworth Art Gallery, University of Manchester

be and grants a framework in space and time in which one can orient oneself, that is, find one's way.

Applying the model to the individual would mean facing the unknown (the seemingly chaotic) and attempting to differentiate it with our conscious faculties. We distinguish the elements, organize them, analyse them, trying to comprehend, to seize their significance as a whole. In such a way we do, in fact, bring light to darkness and find dry land on which to stand. Where the unconscious, chaotic confusion of the waters reigned, the light of consciousness enters. A new order can be evolved; previously unconscious material can be integrated.

We can best understand the significance of this approach by comparing it with that of Apsu. Killing the children so that we can sleep means trying to do away with whatever is bothering us, repressing or suppressing that which seems to cause disorder in our lives. But in that way we are simultaneously destroying the children, vital elements which can lead to further development. Stagnation and rigidity are the result: the creation of a new world is blocked, rendered impossible.

Marduk's chaos confrontation is exemplary and symbolically applicable to the individual in all but one point. His monumental primal ordering of chaos is an eternal event of everlasting import. Once he has created the world from the *massa confusa*, it is there forever. No subsequent chaos encounters are necessary. Human life, on the contrary, goes on, ever-changing, continually bringing new problems, new situations in which chaos erupts. For us, a once in a lifetime chaos encounter is decidedly not enough.

The Babylonians themselves seem to have realized the real human necessity of repeatedly meeting chaos. For, once a year, in the context of their New Year's festivities, called the 'Akitu', they recited the *Enuma Elish*. The purpose was fourfold. First, it was a ritual of transition, meant to guarantee safe passage from the old year to the new. Second, as the ceremony took place in the springtime, when the Euphrates used to overflow its banks, it was a way of recalling the exemplary way Marduk dealt with the chaotic waters. Third, it served to reinvest the king with Marduk's powers. As his earthly representative, thus reinvigorated, the king would be equipped to handle any chaotic situations which might threaten the nation in the year to come. And, fourth, one can well imagine that the people themselves drew strength from the reminder of Marduk's deeds. The example of his heroic ordering of chaos in the beginning could support them in their own, personal chaos encounters in the new year.

But, chaos generally erupts more frequently than once a year, and the Polynesians are well aware of this fact. They draw on their exemplary chaos confrontation whenever it feels necessary. The people then perform rites in which the original words of Io – as he created the light of the world – are repeated. The occasion may be anything from feelings of desperation, sterility, war, or a difficult moment in the creative process. Hare Hongi, a Polynesian whom Mircea Eliade quotes on these ritual usages of Io's words, says that the Polynesians recall the divine formula in any and all situations which 'drive the people to desperation' (Eliade 1977) that is, when chaos threatens their life. The thought of Io's primal ordering, which brought forth light from darkness, helps his believers in their moments of darkness. Their god's words give the Polynesians strength to face chaos.

The ritual remembrance of a divine chaos encounter is widespread. As we shall see at the end of this chapter, we too practise ceremonies in which we recall such an encounter. The ubiquitousness of these rituals indicates the importance of the model. The central idea that the light of consciousness helps to disperse the darkness of the unknown (the unconscious) is a basic element of the nature of *homo sapiens*. But chaos is often so overwhelming in its extent and its darkness that we tend to forget the 'divine' powers of consciousness. That is why institutionalized ceremonies periodically reminded people of their god-given capacities to disperse chaos.

But there is also another approach, this one more feminine, more accepting. It is clearly less active, as it does not rely on the powers of discrimination. But it is based on equally important characteristics of human nature: the capacity to accept and to be moved. In our first example we shall rather see the acceptance of chaos, its valorization, as the determining factor in the encounter.

The fairy tale, 'The Devil's Three Golden Hairs' shows how the mere belief in the power of the chaotic is sufficient to sow the seeds of the solution to a chaotic situation. This situation is well summarized in the three questions about the state of the kingdom which are posed to the hero along his way: why a tree which used to bear golden apples no longer has a single leaf; why a fountain from which wine used to flow has completely dried up; and why the ferryman who crosses over from the kingdom to hell is never relieved from his duties.

The hero, who manages to find the answers to the questions and finally marries the king's daughter, is not gifted with any particularly heroic traits. Nor does he apply his conscious powers to any direct confrontation of the problems at hand. Instead, he confides in the Devil's grandmother: she gets the answers for him from the Devil. She also plucks from the Devil's head the three golden hairs which the king has asked the boy to fetch.

What makes the boy a hero is his special birth and the way it is regarded by the common folk. He was born with a cowl on, that is, with the amniotic sack still around him. This birth, practically non-existent today and rare at any time, is a fluke of nature. As such, it was popularly believed to be a sign of luck. And so it is foretold that when the boy is 13 he will marry the king's daughter.

We need not go into a detailed account of the tale. What interests us is the people's attitude towards the fluke of nature, towards the abnormal birth; it actually provides the key to the chaos encounter. Because the birth is considered 'extra-ordinary', the boy is automatically enabled to remedy the chaotically sterile, fruitless, and stagnating state of the kingdom. He can make the fountain flow again, the tree bloom, and have the ferryman relieved of his duties. He becomes the new king and the representative of a new order. And he can accomplish all of this because he believes in the prediction and quite naturally accepts his role as representative of the abnormal. As such he is close to that which is outside of the norm. He therefore does not hesitate to communicate with this realm and its other representatives. He confides in the Devil's grandmother: she finds the solution to the problems for him.

The abnormal, the accidental, the extra-ordinary, all of that which does not fit into the regular, customary, established order, everything that does not conform to the norm – all of this belongs to the realm of chaos. The popular belief in the special powers of the chaotic is an inherent aspect of all superstition, of folk wisdom, such as we find in this tale. It is still widespread among us today. We need merely think of the way we regard the number thirteen: the erratic number, it falls out of the unit twelve which is seen as a totality. Twelve units count up to a whole dozen; thirteen is no longer a dozen. There are twelve fruits on the tree of knowledge, twelve tribes of Israel, twelve signs of the zodiac. Twelve is a whole unit; thirteen goes beyond it, falls out of it. It is therefore thought to have special, magical powers. This point deserves further reflection, for it helps to explain the tragic fate of minority groups. The very fact of their being different leads to their being seen in a 'special' light. And, depending on the climate of the times, that specialness can be judged as positive or negative. The minority group is praised or persecuted for its special gifts. Persecution of minorities thus seems to have archetypal roots.

Superstition generally tends to valorize the chaotic. Appreciating it as something 'peculiar' and accepting it as such creates a new situation. Whatever is abnormal or different becomes invested with special, extraordinary powers.

Innerpsychically such an attitude is extremely valuable. Think of the way birth marks are considered. When a child is born with such a mark, for example, on the face, its parents are often quite disturbed. The mark destroys the perfect order of the regular, normal face. If, however, it comes to be seen as a 'beauty mark' (as it is also known in English), then it can turn into a distinctive trait of the person. It individualizes him, setting him apart, making him a bit different from other people. It can make him feel special, not 'abnormal'. In the Old Testament special power is attributed to the blemish; that is the reason why only perfect, unblemished animals could be offered up for sacrifice. The power of the blemished animal was thought to interfere with the supreme power of God.

So, it all depends on the point of view. The more we are attached to a certain, conventional image of order, the more disturbing the idea of its disruption. Once the birth mark becomes a beauty mark it is no longer a negative chaos experience, but a vitalizing one.

In the same vein we can understand the particular ugliness that has become the trademark of certain movie stars. Supposedly, when Joseph von Sternberg discovered Marlene Dietrich, she was a rather plain-looking woman, not especially ugly, not especially pretty. He accentuated her big mouth, thus, making her look less ordinary. Millions of movie fans came to admire her 'special type of beauty'. She became a different-looking woman.

This attitude towards the different, the chaotically abnormal is particularly well illustrated by a West African tribe, the Lobis. They practise the custom of placing little statues (see Figure 2.3) in the shrines of their gods, the *thilas*. The statues are meant to persuade the *thilas* to intervene on their behalf when bad luck happens to cross their path. Different kinds of statuettes are used. One kind, for example, is called the '*ti puos*', the dangerous people. They

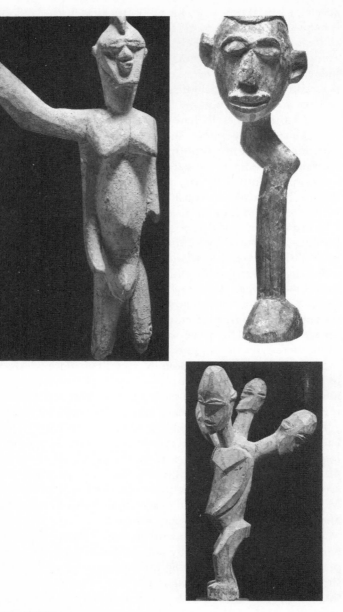

Figure 2.3   Lobis
Source: Meyer (1981)

hold up their arms as if they were defending themselves. Most powerful of all are the '*ti balas*', the unusual people. The Lobis turn to them as a last resort, for example, when their luck is very bad and nothing else has worked. The *ti balas*' magic is extremely potent, for they have very peculiar forms. Their bodies are fashioned with one arm, or three legs, two heads, etc. Because they are different, representing the chaotic, the extra-ordinary, their power goes beyond the ordinary too. This perspective: abnormal = extra-ordinary is an integral aspect of the Lobis' view of life.

Judaism knows a similarly impressive example that shows how fruitful this attitude can be. In the Old Testament we read that God has promised Abraham that his seed will become a great nation. After this promise many years pass and Sarah has borne Abraham no children. One day, three strangers arrive at Abraham's tent: he welcomes them and has a festive meal prepared. As the strangers are departing, they foretell Sarah's pregnancy. She laughs, for she is well beyond child-bearing. But she does become pregnant and, in her old age, she gives birth to Jacob. As Abraham accepted the strangers, a new nation is born, a new order can evolve.

We can interpret welcoming the stranger as making room for that which is foreign, different, outside of the norm, not part of the reigning order. That means accepting and being open to chaos and to the new possibilities it can stimulate. In this way we grant essential space to the flow of life, to its constant challenge, and not only to the comfortable security of our customary and known order. In Chapter 1, we discussed this attitude in relation to artistic and political movements: Dada, surrealism, the anarchists, and even youth movements of various historical periods. All are based on the fundamental valorization of the power of chaos, such as the Lobis, Abraham, the common folk in our fairy tale, and people in superstitious belief the world over exhibit.

The presence of this accepting attitude is an essential prerequisite for all psychic growth. Without it, no possibility of change, of variation, of development, can be conceived as possible. The individual remains caught in a prison of established values, not daring to examine them or to move beyond them. When a person seeks psychotherapy, that is often where he is. In the course of the therapy the accepting attitude towards chaos and what it can bring must be stimulated. A basic confidence in the positive seeds inherent in chaos and what it represents needs to be built so that the maturational process which has been interrupted can be taken up once again.

Our feminine/accepting model possesses quite different qualities from our masculine/confrontational model. It is, however, an essential complement to the latter. Either one without the other is insufficient. Mere acceptance without some conscious confrontation would lead to a relatively unconscious state in which one is led on, in an unreflecting manner from one chaotic circumstance to the other. On the other hand, mere chaos confrontation without acceptance could easily lead to a defensive, rationalizing attitude in which chaos is ultimately blocked off; chaos cannot be allowed to fertilize the deeper layers, because it is not in itself prized as potentially fruitful. It must be cleared up as soon as possible, shelved, and taken care of. No room can be given for it to take seed.

I shall now examine another tale illustrating the passive acceptance of chaos. The acceptance is so passive as to be unconscious: the heroine allows herself to be moved by chaos, but not before she has put up a good fight. The initial avoidance, together with the emotional nature of the chaos experience, makes the tale a good analogy for the fate of many individual people faced with chaos today.

Snow White is a princess born in complete accord with her mother's wishes: her lips are as red as blood, her skin as white as snow, and her hair black like ebony. This perfect picture of harmony is, however, soon left motherless. The king, her father, remarries and the scene is set for the intervention of chaos in a too perfect world.

The tale tells how Snow White's stepmother, on learning from her mirror that Snow White is 'the fairest in all the land', becomes so envious that she plans to have the girl killed. She sends her off into the forest with a hunter whom she has instructed to murder her, but the hunter lets the princess free. She finds refuge at the house of the seven dwarves who agree to let her stay there if she will keep house for them. So, Snow White tends to the dwarf household, but her stepmother discovers her whereabouts and on three separate occasions visits her in disguise. Each time she offers the girl an object which is meant to kill her: a poisoned comb with which she combs her hair, bodice lacings that she laces up so tight that Snow White suffocates, and finally, an apple which is poisoned. The first two times the dwarves manage to find Snow White in time and to save her. But the last time they are apparently too late. Snow White seems to be dead; but she still looks so beautiful that the dwarves place her in a glass coffin on top of a mountain. A prince comes along and falls so much in love with the dead princess that he has her carried off in her coffin. But, on the way down the mountain, a servant trips and the piece of poisoned apple that was stuck in Snow White's throat is dislodged. She awakens to fall immediately in love with the prince. They marry and live happily ever after. At the wedding the evil stepmother is killed.

I want to consider the fairy tale from the subjective point of view and shall interpret it as if it were an inner process: the story of Snow White and her struggle with the chaotic emotions which befall her. Snow White is evidently a perfect little girl who lives with illusions of harmony and perfection; her appearance and her vanity tell us that much: the comb and bodice lacings are her trap. Snow White's father is hardly mentioned in the tale, but her stepmother plays a central role: she is actually the object of the girl's jealousy and envy. We can take this to mean that Snow White feels (as is often the case with second marriages in real life) that her stepmother stands in the way of her relationship with her father. This leads to the girl's fixating on her father, that is, becoming overly attached to him. The attachment manifests, as in real life, in intense and long-lasting feelings against her father's wife. Thus, Snow White's psychic development is arrested. She remains her father's little princess, yearning deeply for a harmonious relationship with him. She cannot grow up and become interested in another man. However, at the end of the tale Snow White is shaken out of her psychic sleep. She falls in love with the prince: she has finally become a young woman capable of attachment to another man besides her father. As soon as she marries the prince, her stepmother complex – the chaotic feelings of jealousy and envy she has towards this rival for her father's love – automatically disappears.

Let us have a look at Snow White's introduction to chaos and how she deals with it. For her, chaos is represented by the jealousy and envy she feels towards her stepmother. They break into her well-ordered world and wreak havoc. Such emotions are difficult for anyone to deal with. They can really turn one's life upside down, as those who have experienced them so well know. One is plagued by obsessive thoughts that are so shameful that one can hardly admit to them, except perhaps in the greatest privacy, in front of the mirror, as the stepmother is said to do. It is understandably difficult to grant such painfully shaming emotions their adequate place, to accept them as valid parts of one's self. For perfect little Snow White that would be especially difficult.

She tries with all her might to get rid of these feelings, first of all by running away from home and staying with the dwarves. But that does not help her to find the necessary distance from her problem. She just takes it with her, as we see from the fact that the stepmother finds her. (That is, her stepmother complex is still very much alive and active.) At each visit of the disguised stepmother, Snow White tries to erase her unwelcome feelings. First, she combs her hair, putting order into the thoughts and fantasies which grow from her head, but the comb which the stepmother gives her is poisoned and Snow White falls, seemingly dead, to the ground. The dwarves find her and remove the poisoned comb. The next time, she tries to deal with her obsessively negative feelings by suppressing them. With the bodice lacings, the stepmother ties her up so tight that she cannot breathe. That is she 'holds it all in', 'pulls herself together', and 'puts up a good show'. But these desperate efforts at squelching her unacceptable feelings are very destructive: they almost kill her; only the dwarves' last-minute interventions manage to save her: they unlace her and she comes back to life. Not infrequently one finds people in real life reacting like Snow White: they do their utmost to block out awareness of their chaotic feelings, pulling themselves together and erecting facades. This way of dealing with psychic chaos is extremely consuming. In the fairy tale, Snow White spends a great deal of her life's energies in thus trying to avoid dealing with the negative emotions which mean chaos for her. And each time she falls into a death-like faint. Real people, too, can find themselves drained by their defensive struggles. As a result they can also lose consciousness or, physically and mentally exhausted by their efforts, fall ill. The fight against chaos can 'lay one flat', just as it does Snow White. Snow White's final trap seems fatal. She accepts an apple from the disguised stepmother. But she decides to take the prettier side, imagining that the other, less perfect-looking side might be poisoned. Her choice is wrong and well reflects the girl's sad misconception of life: the abnormal, the less than perfect is poisoned. The Lobis would have been able to tell her otherwise. Snow White's attachment to order, to perfection, to harmony leads her to a dead end.

As long as she cannot accept the other side of the apple, that is, as long as she cannot become aware of the fact (the apple symbolizes consciousness, awareness) that the less perfect and harmonious also belong to life, she stagnates in her development. To the less perfect side belong her chaotic emotions; to the perfectly ordered side, her image of an ideal relationship with her father. The latter side corresponds to Snow White's naively pure child-like illusions. It is poisonous for her, but she cannot realize that this is so. The bit of apple seems to kill the naive young princess. She is rendered completely passive and unconscious. Even the dwarves cannot bring her back to life this time. But chaos can, as we shall soon see.

Lying in her coffin at the top of the mountain, she has found peace at last: the fight is over. Snow White is no longer wracked by her violent emotions; she no longer has to defend against them. This is the moment of the most perfect harmony: neither tumult nor change perturb her perfect sleep. She lies there unchanged and unchanging: chaos is banned; order reigns supreme. Snow White 'rests in peace', but she is perfectly lifeless. However, chaos and her passive surrender to it bring the princess back to life. As the prince is having her carried down the mountain in her coffin, a servant's stumbling dislodges the apple. The jarring step – accidental and unpredictable – represents the world of chaos. We can interpret it as Snow White's 'falling' in love, for she awakens from the jolt with feelings of love towards the prince. She is aroused from her death-like sleep by this spontaneous emotional reaction. She has become a young woman who, having allowed herself to be 'carried away' by her feelings (instead of defending against them, as she used to), can notice and be drawn to a young man. Thus, she can look forward to the prince's palace and give up her regressive longings for her father.

In the final solution and reintegration of chaos we recognize real-life processes. Snow White's passive, feminine acceptance of chaos did not come naturally to her: she first put up a good fight, defending against her chaotic feelings as best she could and with great energy. In everyday life, too, the ultimate acceptance of what chaos represents (and it is frequently, as with Snow White, the world of unacceptable emotions) is often only possible after all of one's energies have been expended in defensive measures. Only after all has failed can we bring ourselves to give in to chaos. Sometimes that means falling, falling ill, or experiencing other crushing events. Giving up the fight and surrendering to the powers of chaos means letting go, no longer running away, giving up one's efforts to control, to hold it all in, to pull oneself together, to pretend it is not so. It means surrendering to chaos and allowing oneself to be moved by it. The moment of complete regression is an essential factor that makes the ultimate re-animation and further psychic development possible.

Having done her utmost to avoid chaos, to avoid facing and dealing with her emotional turmoil, Snow White can allow herself to be moved by it. Thus, she can discover the joy and excitement which also belong to chaos. Her story shows how, when chaos is accepted, it can enliven, activate, animate. But, as long as one defends against it, rejecting it, it can lay one flat and drain all of life's energies.

So Snow White, in an extremely passive manner, allows herself to be carried away, to be moved by her feelings, and discovers love and life in the process. But she gets involved with chaos without ever consciously saying 'yes' to it. She does not confront it actively, but merely abandons her frantic efforts to control and avoid it.

This fairy tale is the story of a little girl's painful initiation into womanhood. She comes to accept the world of emotions which she felt but rejected as a child; thus she can integrate her feelings into a mature adult life. The tale tells how the stepmother is killed: this complex is depotentiated as soon as Snow White can find another object of her affections besides her father. Hopefully, she has come to be more tolerant towards her emotions in general, for she will need such tolerance in the future. All partnerships, even those of princes and princesses, know emotional turmoil. Dealing with it can bring new vitality to the couple; whereas, rejecting it inevitably leads to catastrophic results.

This feminine form of chaos encounter, which tends to integrate chaos without consciously confronting it or distinguishing its elements, is found in ritual ceremonies the world over. James Frazer in his classic work on superstition and social order among pre-scientific peoples, *The Golden Bough* (1983: 729), reports on the Hos of north-east India.

Just as the Babylonians developed their ritual New Year's celebration in which they recalled the primal mythical ordering of chaos, the Hos have instituted an annual ceremony in which they collectively integrate chaos – but in a more feminine mode. It takes place in January, at the time of the harvest, and consists of three steps, the last of which is actually chaos-integrative. First of all, a sacrifical offering is made to ward off chaos in the year to come; next, the people chase off a demonic figure representing chaos.

Finally, they indulge in chaos: they consume excessive amounts of food and drink; then follows a phase in which the Hos reverse all of their normal habits. Men treat their wives badly, children and parents mistreat each other, servants berate their masters. Wild sexual orgies follow. The next day, everything returns to normal. But in this annual ritual whatever is otherwise unacceptable is the rule.

The celebration of chaos, as I would like to call it, serves to include this aspect of life as part of the whole. Chaos and chaotic feelings and behaviour are granted a place within society. Such demonstrative behaviour actually robs chaos of its threat. Performed at an extremely important moment in the life of the people – the harvest time – the ritual is meant to protect the Hos from the accidental eruptions of chaos in the year to come. A kind of magic, curing like with like, it recalls the Babylonian and the Lobi practices.

As has probably become apparent from the foregoing, we too perform chaos-integrative ceremonies, although we are seldom aware of their significance. And, like our pre-scientific ancestors, we perform them at dangerous times, at moments of transition. In most modern societies the passage from the old to the new year is marked by bonfires, fireworks, or at least wild partying. Similarly, *fasnacht*, *fasching*, and carnival all mark the passage from winter to spring. The winter solstice celebrated in Guy Fawke's Day, Hallowe'en, Walpurgis night, or All Saints' Day are all days of especially loud or festive – in some way chaotic – behaviour.

All of these celebrations – like April Fool's Day, too – serve to grant chaos a place within our established order of life. In this way, we are unconsciously integrating and valorizing it. We are allowing it space within the bounds of our universe and thus, one might say, paying service to its special powers; we are invoking chaos in order to deter its unpredictable appearance, to make it fruitful and not destructive.

In concluding this exposition of the feminine model of chaos encounter, the enormous variations in reactions must be recalled. The spectrum ranges from passive, unconscious acceptance to active indulgence in chaos. Characteristic of the model is the relative unconsciousness of its use and its integrative aspect. The latter aspect especially lends it a maternal tone, setting it off in strong contrast to the masculine/confrontational model which consciously takes chaos in hand, attacking it in an active way.

Despite the apparent opposition between the two models, they can and have been combined in such a way as to complement each other. In the psychotherapeutic situation we work with just such a combined model. The acceptance of chaos is the indispensable prerequisite of any attempts to confront it, to distinguish its elements, and understand its mechanisms. This first step provides the direct, experiential evidence of what the individual's momentary chaos is all about. Naturally, becoming aware of it means allowing oneself to be moved by it; only on the basis of such an experiential contact can any conscious differentiation take place.

Aquatic initiation rites offer an ancient model for such a combination of the masculine and feminine approaches. Mircea Eliade in his book *Le Sacré et Le Profane* (1975) interprets the Christian baptism in this sense. He sees it as a descent into the water in order to vanquish the dragon of the deep. Supposedly, this is just what Jesus did: he entered the River Jordan to do battle with the dragon Behemoth who, according to Job, dwelt there. The initiate, in Jesus's wake, does the same, imitating Jesus's actions, recalling his primal battle with the dragon. At the same time, through his own immersion in water, he too meets the dragon. He enters into a direct, physical encounter with this reality, allowing himself to be touched by it. And, he emerges with his life's energies thus renewed.

Many other aquatic initiation rites exist in which a divinity serves as a role model in the meeting with the waters. The reminder of his divine capacity to order chaos, plus the initiate's own acceptance of it in the here and now of the immersion, are the two basic elements of all such rites. An essential aspect is the goal of the ritual: the initiate's renewal.

The *mikvah* – the ritual bath in Judaism – which is most likely the original source of the Christian baptism can be interpreted in a similar way. The major differences are the particular mythical act referred to and the way in which the ritual is used. God's creation of the world out of the original undivided waters is the reference point here. And the ritual re-enactment is a repetitive one. Immersion in the *mikvah* marks transition phases in the life of a woman. The first is the passage from childhood to marriage and, subsequently, the monthly passage from one menstrual cycle to the next.

The psychotherapeutic chaos encounter can well be compared with these aquatic rituals. Not only the means of approach, but also the nature of chaos and the goals of the procedure correspond. They are, in fact, symbolically identical. In supporting the individual's willingness and ability to allow himself to be immersed in the water, we are encouraging him to learn to have confidence in it. That which is unknown, and therefore creates chaotic first impressions – the unconscious itself – can become familiar: being touched, being moved by it, can have a positive outcome. It can consequently be approached, examined and dealt with in such a way as to bring differentiation and order to its contents, thus making them less monumentally threatening. The elements integrated into consciousness – that is, which we become aware of – are added to the conscious mind, and therefore enlarge it, making it stronger, more vigorous. The energies of the conscious personality are thus revitalized. In this way an invigorating renewal can take place. Chaos can become a fruitful experience.

In summing up what we have discovered in this chapter we can discern ten major points. First, finding ways to encounter chaos seems to be a universal human need; it has been satisfied in past cultures by ceremonies endowed with mythological significance from which the collective and the individual could draw strength. Second, periodic repetition of the ceremonies is necessary, for chaos can never be dealt with definitively: it erupts again and again in the normal course of ever-changing life circumstances. Third, transition phases are marked by such ceremonies; they are especially dangerous times, for what is to come is as yet unknown and basically unpredictable. This makes new phases especially threatening. In terms of order, the old order cannot encompass the new situation; it merely rejects it as chaotic. Finding a new, more all-embracing order would be essential for life to continue. Here we see that, fourth, chaos is that which is new and different; it does not comply to the normal and expected patterns. It can be considered abnormal or extra-ordinary, depending on one's point of view. The appreciation of chaos as extra-ordinary is – fifth – one aspect of the chaos acceptance model which involves the rather passive, maternally toned, feminine chaos acceptance pattern. Sixth, this pattern seems to be the exact opposite of the masculine chaos confrontation model which attacks the chaotic impressions with the tools of consciousness and tries to dissect them, making them digestible for our conscious minds. However, seventh, in psychotherapy we work with a combination of the two patterns of chaos encounter, combining and varying them to suit the needs of the moment. Eighth, the goal of the work is, as in the aquatic initiation rites which can be seen as a model, the renewal of individuals: they find a new order and gain energies from their wresting unconscious material from the jaws of the dragon.

Ninth, chaos has been represented by a dragon, a monster of the deep, or water. The 'formless void' which we discovered in Chapter 1 has taken on new nuances: it is formless and flowing (water) in contrast with the rigid immobility of order. It can be dangerous in its uncontrolled state (flooding), but if handled in the correct way, it becomes fruitful (the Euphrates irrigates the land and Marduk's mythical ordering of the primal waters creates the universe). In more concrete, human terms, chaos is anything which is undifferentiated or unconscious; it is often the world of emotion whose negative tone stems from the fact that it is rejected. But as soon as it can be accepted and appreciated, it serves to enrich individuals. They can understand it and integrate the formerly unacceptable emotions into their self–image. In this way, chaos becomes fruitful; we feel invigorated by the flow and movement characteristic of it. Finally (tenth), as we have seen, wherever chaos is absent, life becomes static and sterile, and ceases to flow. Integrating chaos leads to the renewal of life itself.

In the next chapter the kind of reactions which characterize human beings faced with chaos will be examined in detail. We shall see the extremes to which order can be carried when it is used as a defence against chaos. And we shall be able to observe the way in which life and life forces, emotional contact with the world at large, and, ultimately, contact with oneself, can be blocked off through the rejection of chaos. The examples chosen all in some way typify spontaneous human reactions. They will both recall the importance of finding adequate ways of dealing with chaos and reveal some of our typical psychological mechanisms in the face of it.

Chapter 3

Individuals in the face of chaos

If in the preceding chapter we have been able to see how different peoples of the past have devoted the energy of their culture to finding satisfying ways of dealing with chaos, we shall see here how difficult it is for individuals to do the same. That is why collective forms of chaos encounter developed: to help the individual deal with this typically human problem.

The pivotal point around which the difference between the individual and the collective facing chaos revolves is the term 'facing'. Individuals tend to do whatever they can to avoid facing chaos. Innumerable and even ingenious measures are developed in order to resist the encounter. That is not to say that certain groups do not also evolve similar defensive measures. The scapegoat mechanism, for example, has been used in many a society as a defence against chaos. When I speak of collective chaos encounters I am referring to examples such as those described in the Chapter 2: chaos is accepted or met instead of being expelled or rejected.

This chapter examines three specific cases of individual people faced with chaos. What chaos is for each and the way each reacts towards it will be the main focus of our interest. Generally speaking, we shall find our preliminary observations confirmed here: in the face of chaos people tend to withdraw and to emphasize order. Examples drawn from literature and from real life help to differentiate this reaction further.

In the first example, Edith, in Patricia Highsmith's *Edith's Diary* (1980) creates an order of her own in a fantasy world. There she seeks refuge from the chaos of her life. But her order proves to be a fatal trap. Edith dies under the weight of her overgrown fantasy world. The next example stems from Turgenev's *Fathers and Sons* (1966) and portrays the inner struggles of Odintsov, a woman who prefers a well-ordered universe to the chaos of emotional turmoil. She rejects love only to fall into incomprehensible depressions. The third example is drawn from real life: it shows how a young schizophrenic constructs a rigid plan of daily activities. The extreme order of his eccentric life does not, however, prevent the outbreak of his psychotic episode a few months later. All of these three people withdraw from what appears to them as chaos; each constructs a system of order apart from and in opposition to their chaotic experience. None manages to find a kind of order which might encompass the chaotic elements which belong to life.

Edith Howland is a housewife and journalist. She is married to Brett and they have one child, Cliffie. He is a difficult little boy who steals and lies; he even tries to smother the family cat but typically, he denies everything and gets away with it. Brett and Edith do not know how to handle the boy. Often when there is a problem with him, they try to ignore it: they change the subject, turn on the television or take a drink. Edith and Brett avoid conflict as much as possible. And so, when Brett comes home one day to announce to Edith that he wants to leave her for his young secretary, Edith gives in without a word. Brett moves out, leaving Edith behind with Cliffie and with his own bed-ridden Uncle George. Edith does her best to cope with all of this. She takes care of George and goes to work to earn a living besides. Cliffie is at home most of the time, generally drunk, and without a job. Despite all of her troubles, Edith tries to keep happy and content, but she is actually filled with bitterness and anger, disappointment and resentment. She had so wanted her life to be otherwise. And so, she pretends to herself that it is. She keeps a diary and one day she begins to make false entries. She writes about how Cliffie has become a successful engineer, graduated from Princeton, how he marries a lovely girl, Debbie, and they have two beautiful children. They write to Edith and come to visit her. Gradually Edith begins to believe what she has made up. Cliffie and Debbie and their two children become so real for her that she actually knits sweaters for the children and cooks a festive dinner for them all. Edith's fantasies press more and more for realization, for concretization. She decides to sculpt busts of the family. She makes Cliffie into a Roman emperor. In the meantime, Brett has become alarmed about Edith's state: friends have told him how strange she has become. He visits her one day in the company of a psychiatrist. When they ask to see her work, Edith decides to carry her bust of Cliffie downstairs to them. She trips and falls and dies immediately. Her fantasies have become so weighty that they outweigh her reality. And that was the sense of them anyway.

Edith defines her personal chaos – and actually that of most people – in one succinct phrase: 'The difference between dream and reality is the true hell' (p. 265). It is this difference between her imagination of how things should be and how they actually are that 'drives her to desperation', as the Polynesians would say.

Peace and harmony belong to Edith's image of the 'natural order' of things: she wanted to name her house 'Peace'. When, however, she must come to realize that her life does not really correspond to this image, she distances herself from reality and flees into her dreams. A quasi-automatic mechanism develops. Whenever Edith is painfully touched by the disappointing contrast between reality and her dreams, she seeks refuge in her diary. She runs upstairs to her work-room and confides to her diary some new and exciting event – untrue, of course – in which she takes pride and pleasure. She is continually at work on building up this dream world. With time she comes to believe it is real.

Edith fixates on Cliffie as the main cause of her desperation. The day on which he is disqualified at his college entrance examinations marks the beginning of her retreat into her diary. Cliffie's successful life is the major content of the fantasies Edith paints for herself. Actually, he is merely the extension of herself. His success means her success; the joy and happiness of his life makes Edith's own life worth living.

But on one occasion she actually becomes aware of a principal element of her chaos. The experience which she spends so much of her life's energies trying to avoid is prompted by Aunt Melanie. This beloved aunt is making one of her regular visits at the time when Brett has announced that he wants to leave Edith. Aunt Melanie discusses the situation with her niece and tries to persuade her to face it and to act accordingly: she should let Brett know that she still loves him and does not want him to leave. Thus forced to look her marital crisis in the face, Edith has a vision of chaos. It appears to her as 'an abyss beneath her, black and dangerous' (p. 111) (such visions often mark a chaos experience, as the etymological roots – emptiness, chasm – indicate).

> She had a sense of empty time, lots of time, years, months, days, evenings. She was reminded more strongly [. . .] than when she had written the sentence maybe twenty years ago, that life really had no meaning, for anyone, not merely herself. But if she herself were alone, was going to be alone, then the meaninglessness was going to be that much more terrifying.   (p .111)

Fear of leading a meaningless life alone: this is the bottom line of Edith's fears: it is the prime motivation for her defensive manoeuvres. In order to avoid this most terrible of all fates, she must avoid conflict. She cannot allow her own conflictual feelings to surface: they could reveal her dissatisfaction and tempt her to do something about it. She could end up living a meaningless life alone. Better pretend that all is well, then there is no danger that her nightmares will come true.

Edith is marked by a profound chaos intolerance. Whatever does not meet up with her expectations for herself and her life is unacceptable and must be rejected. The difference between her expectations and reality (dream and reality) is, as she says, 'pure hell' (p. 265). Chaos and order are completely irreconcilable in her psyche. She can only accept and believe in order and must exclude anything that feels chaotic.

In such a dead–end position Edith formulates the equation: order = sanity. And she holds fast to her precept, first trying to apply it concretely to reality. She keeps her house in very good order for quite a while, but with time, this outer reality loses its importance for her. She begins to neglect it and to devote more and more time and energy to her dreams. She keeps order mainly with the help of her imagination. She imagines that Cliffie's messy room is just not part of her house. She escapes into music: 'a world of beauty and brilliance with a beginning and an end' (p. 265), as she describes it. And she flees into the ordered world of her diary. The real, conflictual world which surrounds her she tries to ignore, to gloss over, to diminish in importance. So, she reaches for alcohol and cigarettes whenever a conflict stares her in the face. This helps her to turn her attention away from whatever might be bothering her. She also trivializes her problems: when Brett tries to help her, she compares her situation to the much more serious plight of the Vietnamese, the starving millions, or even the President of the

United States. All of these defensive gestures are meant to help Edith pretend to herself that everything is all right. But they are escapes from her painful reality and contribute to her emotional withdrawal from it.

In the pages of her diary, Edith actually creates order: Is she not in this way acting as Marduk did? No, she is not, for Edith avoids accepting and facing chaos. Her order is constructed not out of chaos but in opposition to it. This makes it unviable, for, as we have seen, chaos contains the seeds of life. Further growth and development are impossible as long as Edith holds on to this static order. And, thus, her death comes to pass. Carrying her bust of Cliffie downstairs, Edith stumbles. Chaos enters through the accidental step (just as it did in 'Snow White'), but Edith cannot let go of her order (and its monumental portrait). Pulled down by its weight, she falls down the flight of stairs and dies.

This heroine is in many ways similar to Snow White, who also held onto a rigid order and rejected chaos. But, whereas the fairy tale princess could finally let go and submit to being moved, Edith cannot. The fall is too far – the distance between dream and reality is too great. Also like 'Snow White' is Edith's complete denial of her emotions. She wants to be happy and content and cannot deal with the pangs of disappointment with her life, or with Cliffie. We might say that Edith cannot consciously suffer. She cannot allow herself be touched by emotion. She is unable to bear emotional turmoil. This basic human capacity is lacking in Edith's personality. And so, whenever she senses sadness, anger, bitterness, disappointment come over her, she withdraws from it and turns to her make-believe world of joy and happiness. It is as if she then turned off her receptors for pain and pretended that peace and harmony reigned.

Like many of her real life counterparts, Edith manages to find small, inappropriate outlets for her nonetheless virulent emotions. She lets out her anger in acerbic newspaper articles against the government. Her deep sadness finds expression in mourning for the death of her cat. These outlets are acceptable for her. Windows to reality, they serve as vents for all of those pent-up feelings which she cannot otherwise allow herself to feel. They play an important role in her psychic household.

Edith's withdrawal into a world of fantasy is a well-known and widely practised form of chaos avoidance. Recent history provides us with a large-scale example of this mechanism at work: the flourishing of the film industry during the Great Depression. At that time millions flocked into the glamorous space of the moving picture theatres to take part in a 'world of brilliance with a beginning and an end', to put it in Edith's own words. The theatres, designed as exotic palaces, featured a fairy tale atmosphere of films, stars, and starlets in which people in economic despair took pleasure. The world of order and meaning in which they participated whole-heartedly for an hour or so offered solace for the chaos of their impoverished lives.

The basic difficulty of this type of avoidance pattern is that it makes chaos and order absolute terms which are completely distinct from each other and, hence, irreconcilable. Chaos is what drives one to despair; it evokes unpleasant feelings. It must be avoided. Order is the world of dream and fantasy in which one can revel. Its harmony and peace are extreme and illusory. The emotional withdrawal from the one, combined with the investment in the other makes for a pat situation. Neither world can fertilize the other; no change can be foreseen, for both images are staid and frozen.

The order which characterizes Edith's world, as well as those candy cotton fantasy worlds, is a rigid, unrealistic order. No room is left for grey tones, only pure whites exist. This is a deathly, rigid order which restricts the individual's capacity to adapt realistically to the greys that make up the ground tone of the picture of life.

The importance of emotional dynamics in such a process cannot be sufficiently emphasized. The unacceptability of certain emotions is the cornerstone of all chaos rejection. Mainly it is disappointment with the difference between ideal images and reality which is unbearable. When we are incapable of suffering from disappointment we tend to reject the chaotic clash of dream and reality. We feel the need to retreat, to withdraw, and to protect ourselves from realizing and feeling our pain.

And so, when in desperation, face to face with chaos, we want to flee and find refuge in fortresses of order. Edith's personal fortress was a construction of her own invention: a fantasy world in which there was room for only the good, the joyful, and the fulfilling. Such a supremely 'meaningful' world as Edith made up is, however, illusory. The total absence of conflict in it was, as we have seen, a much needed compensation for the very conflictual reality which she felt closing in around her. Edith's fantasy fortress was a castle in the sky which was meant to make her forget the miserable hovel she was living in. And the castle was, therefore, too remote, too perfect, too glorious and pure: beside it nothing was valid. Nothing counted. Such exclusive order is always dangerous, as its claims of perfection and harmony deny the reality of life.

Before leaving Edith, it is important to note that fantasy worlds are not always refuges from chaos and fortresses of order. On the contrary, they can sometimes be 'chaotic corners'. Some people can only live out their needs for chaos in split-off fantasy worlds. I am thinking here of a young man whose extremely controlled existence left no room for mistakes, nor for spontaneity or creative experimentation. But he had a habit which made his life livable: he used to withdraw periodically into very wild fantasies. There he could take off on adventurous journeys with exciting people. The outcome was never quite certain: the excitement of the unpredictable reigned supreme. A main goal of therapy was to bring these two separate worlds closer together, to render chaos and order less oppositional. This meant trying to integrate elements of chaos and fantasy within the boundaries of the young man's everyday life.

Let us now turn to an example of a flight into order, but this time into the order of a well-organized life. Turgenev's Russian princess, Anna Sergeyevna exemplifies this frequent phenomenon in his novel *Fathers and Sons*. Odintsov, as she is also known, is the rich and beautiful daughter of a renowned gambler and member of the Czarist nobility. She lives according to an order that is as exclusive as Edith's: it excludes chaotic emotions. As a result, Odintsov's life is clearly impoverished; cut off from her feelings, this woman is consequently plagued by depressive states which she seeks to lighten by committing herself ever more deeply to her well-run, but emotionally empty life.

Fathers and Sons tells the story of the impossible love which grows between Odintsov and Bazarov, an adamant nihilist. The novel opens as Bazarov and his friend Arkady meet Odintsov who invites them for a stay at her country house. They take up the invitation and during their visit, Bazarov and Odintsov evidently fall in love. But when he reveals his love to her, Odintsov rejects him, denying any mutual feelings. Bazarov leaves. Much later on he comes to see her again and she tells of the depression that she fell into after his departure. It took some time for her to regain her balance again, but she did manage to do so. Not long after, Bazarov dies: a medical student, he dissects a typhus-infected cadaver without gloves and

Figure 3.1a   Movie theatre in Atlanta (the hallway)
Source: McCall, John Clark, Jr. (1975) Atlanta Fox Album: Mecca at Peach Tree Street, Footprint Company, Atlanta, Georgia

Figure 3.1b   Inside movie theatre in Atlanta
Source: see Figure 3.1a

Figure 3.2   Tuschinski movie theatre, Amsterdam

is infected by the bacteria. Odintsov marries a lawyer with whom she lives a passionless life. Odintsov's life can be characterized by a phrase that Bazarov uses with disdain, 'life on rails' (p. 71). That is, she lives according to a compulsively organized timetable which she follows unswervingly. Nothing is left to chance, to spontaneity; nothing is unstructured, unplanned. During their stay with her, Bazarov and Arkady are obliged to follow her prescribed plan of activities. At eight o'clock tea is served. Then the guests have a free period until lunch while Odintsov is occupied with her bailiff, her butler, and her housekeeper. Before dinner, conversation or reading is on the schedule – for everyone. Evenings are spent either in taking walks, playing cards, or listening to music. Bed-time is at half-past ten.

This 'ostentatious punctuality' (p. 71), as Bazarov calls it, gives the impression that Odintsov has everything under control. He tells her that she has 'ordered her existence with such impeccable regularity that there can be no place in it for dullness or sadness . . . for any unpleasant emotions' (p. 76). Of course, this is the goal, the unconscious motivation, for Odintsov's life on rails: it is meant to keep emotional turmoil, the unexpected, the uncontrollable, and the chaotic at bay.

But Odintsov is potentially a passionate woman who lives a life defended against her feelings. Turgenev comments: 'had she not been rich and independent, she would perhaps have thrown herself into the struggle and have known passion' p. 70. She is also an imaginative person, but when her dreams and fantasies die away 'she [does] not regret them' (p. 70). An intimate scene reveals Anna Sergeyevna's truly sensitive nature. In it she is in the bath. As she steps out, a breeze sends a chill through her and she shrinks 'into herself, and feels plaintive and almost angry, and there was only one thing she cared for at that instant – to get away from that horrid draught' (p. 70). Odintsov gives others the impression that she is eternally and supremely calm and controlled. In reality, a breeze is enough to ruffle this heroine. It is, therefore, understandable that she tries to retain 'a hold' on herself and her life by adhering to such meticulously ordered activity.

From this perspective we can also understand that when she meets her antithesis, Bazarov, she must fall in love with him. And it is also quite clear that she cannot allow herself to do so. When Bazarov openly expresses his feelings for her, Anna Sergeyevna bluntly refuses him, but not without an inner struggle. She immediately draws away from his passionate embrace, protesting that he has misunderstood her. But, as soon as he leaves the room, she senses her confusion. She catches a glimpse of herself in her mirror: 'her head thrown back, with a mysterious smile on the half-closed, half-opened eyes and lips, told her, it seemed in a flash, something at which she herself was confused' (p. 83). Odintsov's feelings are evidently not at all as clear as they sounded when she refused Bazarov. But, faced with chaotic confusion, Odintsov consciously decides in favour of peace and order, as she says to herself. 'No . . . God knows what it would lead to; you can't toy with him; peace is the best thing in the world anyway' (p. 83). Opting for peace and order, harmony and calm is typical for her: indulging her emotions, letting herself go is far from Odintsov's mind and abilities. Her fear of chaos and what it might lead to is too great to allow her to accept being moved by emotion.

Turgenev leaves no doubt that it is chaos which Odintsov fears. He portrays her, as Patricia Highsmith portrayed Edith in a similar situation, faced with the image of chaos itself. As she imagines getting involved in a relationship with Bazarov, the formless void appears before her inner eye: 'she had forced herself to go up to a certain point, forced herself to go behind it, and had seen not even an abyss, but a void . . . or something hideous' (p. 83). Allowing her feelings to take over would mean chaos for Odintsov. Frightened by such a prospect, she must refuse. Were she to accept, she would be faced with formlessness. The accidental, the unexpected could gain a hold on her life. And the order and control which she aims for with the 'ostentatious punctuality' of her 'life on rails' (p. 71) would be endangered, if not flatly destroyed. Bazarov and her feelings for him are a serious danger for Anna Sergeyevna and her repressed passionate nature.

Although she seems to manage very well in suppressing her romantic attraction for Bazarov, under her veneer Odintsov goes through difficult moments. Turgenev describes them for us. Just after the scene in question, she feels definitely uncomfortable about seeing her guests again: 'Though Odintsov's self-control was great, and superior as she was to every kind of prejudice, she felt awkward when she went into the dining room to dinner' (p. 84). After dinner, Bazarov apologizes to her: 'She did not answer him. "I'm afraid of this man," flashed through her brain' (p. 84).

When Bazarov comes to pay a visit some time later, she receives him, but not without 'an involuntary sense of tension' (p. 141) and a deep sigh. On this occasion she tells him about the 'fit of depression' (p. 141) that she had had after his last visit. Not understanding what it was all about, she had made plans to go abroad. But, with the passage of time, she fell 'back into her old routine' (p. 142).

Distraction from herself, from the matters of her heart and from the moods that proceed from them (achieved by adhering to the regular train of her life) help Odintsov to recover. She nevertheless carries the scars on her being. Continually checking her natural impulses, avoiding any changes in her programme, she cuts herself off from the flow and fire of life. Odintsov lives in a well-ordered, well-distracted way in a comfortable, but essentially inanimate universe. Order and harmony, perfection and stability, are what count for her; the cost is vitality. This woman makes her choices, but they pull her down again and again into depressive states that she neither wills nor comprehends. Seemingly in control of herself and her emotional life, Odintsov is actually the victim of her emotions and of these depressions that 'come upon her "goodness knows why"', as she says (p. 141).

Psychologically speaking, her depressions are a quite natural reaction to the suppressed life within. Not acting out her impulses does not make them less real. Smothered, they continue to live within her, but in a way that frustrates the development of a satisfied personality.

Turgenev does not leave us up in the air about Odintsov's fate. It is as to be expected. Long after Bazarov dies, she marries a successful lawyer who is 'cold as ice' and they 'live in the greatest harmony together' (p. 164). What else could we imagine from the woman who stated that 'peace is the best thing in the world' (p. 83)? As both she and her husband live estranged from their emotions, they can easily achieve harmony.

The case of Odintsov serves as a real, human and individual counterpart to Snow White. Whereas, the fairy tale princess could with time come to give up her efforts to uphold a facade and to suppress her violent emotions, the Russian princess remains stuck in her defensive position. The order of her life continues to provide security for her in the face of chaos. Odintsov never manages to let go and allow herself to be 'moved'. Instead, she pursues her suppression, her energy-consuming defensive manoeuvres which inevitably lead to depression and emotional emptiness.

Odintsov's fate calls to mind a woman who came to see me

because of depressions. She, too, had fallen in love. She, too, held fast to a conception of order that meant a great deal to her. She belonged to a strict religious group with very clear rules and regulations about what was right and what was wrong. She had done her best until now to follow what was required of her, but now she was in desperation, for she had fallen in love with a man who was entirely unacceptable to her group. The thought of a relationship with him was impossible. She had to give up any hopes in this direction. And so, she had broken off all contact with him and had fallen into a deep depression.

During our work together, this woman's strong attachment to her religious order needed to be more clearly understood. For it was associated with compelling rules which had now begun to make her life difficult. She was evidently in a state of inner conflict between her need for the order and meaning which the group and its beliefs offered and her present need for emotional involvement in a loving relationship. She came to realize that her choice of affiliation with this religious group had grown out of a deep longing for security. The conflict which had now arisen permitted her to ask herself important questions about this security, if it was still so necessary for her, and if it might not be satisfied by other means. Evidently, something in her had already sensed that this strong religious attachment was out of date; otherwise, she could not have fallen in love with a man of whom her group could not possibly approve.

As we hinted in introducing Odintsov, her basic attitude is far from uncommon. Many people enter therapy with similar expectations: they want to be able to control themselves and their emotions. And they attempt to do so in the same way as Odintsov did. They want to 'keep the show going' without anyone noticing that there is anything wrong. They do not want to be bothered by intense feelings. 'Life on rails' must continue; its proper, well-oiled functioning is of utmost concern. And, especially, those silly, unwanted, unexpected, and completely incomprehensible symptoms must be made to disappear as soon as possible, because they really do get in the way of going along with the business of life as usual.

Odintsov is a fictional character, yes, but she incorporates so much of what modern human beings carry with them – their fears, their hopes, their needs and their expectations – that she stands out in an exemplary manner. 'Life on rails' is replaced today, more than a hundred years after Odintsov's creation, by life on course, at jet-propelled speed. We have achieved greater speed, and the tendency has led to greater expectations of competence. Personal efforts to control are aided and abetted by the tools of progress: countless types of therapy, diagnostic apparatus, and medicinal products. 'Life on rails' has become industrialized on a large scale so that temporary states of being 'out of whack', 'out of *order*' (as we say) can be speedily transformed.

Chaos for Odintsov has to do with emotions: she fears the turmoil that could be stirred up in her placid atmosphere. She defends against it by denying her feelings and suppressing them. The results, perhaps not as extreme as Edith's, are her depressive states that combine with a general feeling of the purposelessness of life. She cannot erase this discomfort, but by keeping active and busy she manages to compensate for the emptiness, the senselessness. Edith built herself an 'Ersatz reality' that kept her busy.

Busy-ness is a characteristic trait of our modern society's defences. Approved collectively as a justified and highly acceptable state of being, busy-ness helps to keep things in order. For, when one so arranges life as to have no time to reflect, then one can avoid dealing with problems, conflicts, chaos, whatever might disturb the slick surface of appearances.

An amazing number of people today have never had the time nor even the idea of being quiet, unoccupied, and alone. This is why so many, when they must be home sick, for example, get very nervous and jittery, can hardly wait to get up and be 'on the go' again. Solitude and silence are rarities which can evoke abysmal reactions; being busy and staying busy is one of the Western world's main defences against the abyss.

Our literary examples have provided us with detailed psychological portraits of two women whose fear of chaos and flight into order reveal definite similarities. The main difference is that Edith flees into a fantasized order of her own invention; whereas Odintsov flees into structured activities. As we have mentioned, both women, although fictional, have their counterparts among us.

Next an example from real life will be examined. It is an almost caricature version of Odintsov's 'life on rails'. The rather eccentric and very intensely filled timetable in Table 3.1 stems from the prodromes of the mental illness known as schizophrenia. It, too, shows how a person flees from chaos into the arms of order. The emotional withdrawal from the world at large which we have observed in the preceding literary examples is once again the prime motivation for the flight into strict order. Singular here is the extraordinary rigidity of the order: it is immediately apparent.

The young man who drew up the timetable was 19 years old at the time. Three months later he was admitted to a psychiatric hospital in an acute catatonic state. That is, he had a schizophrenic attack in which his body was rigid, perhaps even immobile.

As the psychiatry textbook from which the timetable is drawn provides no further details, we do not know exactly what triggered the young man's state. However, the timetable itself tells us a great deal about what he must have been experiencing at the time when he undertook to organize his life thus. From what is left out of the activities we can surmise what he wanted to avoid: free time, contact with people, any emotional jolts and all unexpected impressions from without or within. What he evidently needed to reinforce was his own sense of being in control. This is evident both in the form

Table 3.1

Time	Activity
7:00–8:00	cold bath, wash, bed, dress
8:00–8:15	encyclopaedia (memorize three things)
8:15–8:30	hand written things
8:30–8:45	brisk walk
8:45–9:00	breakfast (1 apple, 1 piece bran bread, 2 glasses milk, 2 glasses water)
9:00–10:00	listen, look, smell
10:00–11:00	news (Europe, economy, sport)
11:00–12:00	wax floors and clean door handles
12:00–13:00	cold bath and gymnastics
13:00–13:30	geometry
13:30–13:45	vegetable meal (light and digestible)
13:45–14:45	music
14:45–15:45	walk to monument and then back to library
15:45–17:00	library work
17:00–18:00	book-keeping
18:00–18:20	cold bath
18:20–18:35	vegetable meal
18:35–20:05	book-keeping
20:05–21:00	listen, look, smell
21:00–21:30	health magazine
21:30–22:00	wardrobe
22:00–22:20	cold bath
22:20–22:40	learn vocables (12 words)
22:40–23:00	undress and wash
23:00–23:15	breathing exercise
23:15–23:30	recording of progress of mental powers during day

Source: Lehmann (1984)

and content of the schedule. It is extremely tight. Nothing is left to chance. Nothing is left unguarded or open. The entire day from early morning to late night is planned in great detail. The small units of time – from ten to fifteen minutes, at most an hour – are like a thickly meshed net constructed to safeguard his fall into the looming abyss. Allowing no empty spaces, no room for inactivity precludes those empty moments in which one might otherwise daydream, muse, or in which doubts and fears could arise. As we saw in regard to Odintsov's busy life, the lack of time to reflect, to be diverted from life's activities, is characteristic of our age and, like this rather extreme schedule, often serves defensive purposes.

The young man's attempts to feel 'on top of it' are also reflected in the content of his daily activities. What he has drawn up here is a total fitness plan which follows the Roman *mens sana in corpore sano* formula. The young man trains his mind – learning words, memorizing bits from the encyclopaedia. At the same time, he trains his body by taking brisk walks and doing physical exercise. He nourishes his body with vegetables, milk, and whole wheat products; he nourishes his mind with learning and with music. Such exaggerated concern for fitness – so prevalent in contemporary society – can, like exaggerated busy-ness, be used as a defence against chaos. Sensing that something is not quite right, one applies one's energies to the practical goal of fitness. One trains mind and body with the unconscious goal of silencing the voices that make themselves heard. And so, as fat and flab are exercised away, the shadowy qualities, the whispering doubts and fears are meant to be chased away. The defensive motivation for the activity is often revealed by its caricature-like features.

The schedule's stress on broadening and deepening awareness is significant. This was apparently the main intent of the young man as he drew up his schedule, for at the end of each day he plans to 'note the progress of mental powers'. It is within this context that we can understand the time and energy he devotes to the conscious exercise of those functions which are otherwise involuntary and unconscious: smelling, seeing, and hearing.

It seems that the young man felt threatened, endangered, and did all he could to get a hold on things. He tried to become very aware, to disperse the dark and ominous clouds he felt closing in on him. And he tried to strengthen himself for the battle. Marduk's confrontation with Tiamat was very consciousness-oriented. The desire to become ever more conscious could be understood as preparation for the confrontation with the monsters of the deep.

However, as we saw with Edith, chaos is not confronted, but rather avoided. All of the man's efforts are concentrated on focusing the beam of consciousness *away* from the dark corners. The main movement is not directed toward chaos but away from it. We sense very distinctly how he retreats and sets up a world of his own, apart from the common world of human experience. One can say that he creates his own universe, a place where things go according to his own wishes. This refuge is characterized by extreme order and a private meaningfulness. Here the young man tries to live, to get a sense of being in control of his fate. Here he tries to pretend that chaos does not exist. There is no room for desperation in this overly busy and secluded world. Here is the security of the known, the light of consciousness. Or that is the intent, at any rate.

There is a slight hint that the young man already felt the pangs of chaos in a feverish emotional state: he prescribes cold baths for himself. Like the more recent shock treatments, cold baths used to belong to the treatment of schizophrenic states. The cold shock of water on a feverish system brings down the excitement and the temperature. Is this what the man was trying to accomplish with his plan? Withdrawal from the heat of emotional excitement in favour of a colder and more distanced approach to life and knowledge can be symbolized by the cold water treatment. In terms of our image of being moved by chaos, we can say that the entire concentration is on *not* being moved, on counteracting the effects of chaos. The driving need here is the construction of a bulwark against the impending danger of being overwhelmed. But, despite all of his concentrated efforts, the young man does not seem to have been able to ward off chaos. The catatonic state into which he fell is the ultimate concretization of the timetable. The retreat from reality has become so extreme, the young man has become so withdrawn emotionally – so autistic – that he finally becomes completely inflexible, unmoveable. He has done his best to avoid being moved by chaos but, nevertheless, he is overwhelmed.

This type of paradoxical development is not rare. When the defence against chaos reaches its peak, chaos often erupts. The extreme order seems to snap and its opposite appears. Anorexics offer an example of such a paradoxical development. Their eating-vomiting strategies are efforts at controlling and ordering: they thus try to keep their weight under control and, at the same time, to keep unconscious conflicts out of sight and mind. However, when their order becomes too intense, too rigid, they suddenly fly off into chaotic activity: their impulses become uncontrollable. They are then subject to eating 'binges', known as bulimic attacks, during which they eat everything in sight. The order and control with which they constantly try to ward off the uncontrollable fail completely and they are faced with chaos. Similar rebound effects can be observed in phobias.

Another well-known phenomenon which is illustrated both in the timetable and in the young man's subsequent catatonic state is the rigidification that finds its expression in the body. In this case, the young man became immobile. Schizophrenic patients manifest varying degrees of physical rigidity. But, also people who are in no way schizophrenic can demonstrate similar physical symptoms in, for example, rigid posture, a stiff neck. Stiffness and rigidity of the body have to do with fear. When we are afraid, we stiffen up; the expression 'petrified with fear' puts it well. This is a physiological fact: our muscles, but also our skin becomes taut. We get 'goose bumps'. Sometimes we really feel 'the hair standing on our heads'. Cats and other animals have bristling hairs in moments of particular danger. And we may well wonder if their stiffening up and 'playing dead' is not identical to our feeling 'paralysed' with fear. We also know the reaction of trying to counteract our fears by 'steeling ourselves' for a fight. Some people who feel especially insecure tell of how they try to 'gird' themselves up, seeking a strong physical position in frightening situations. Intra-psychically, too, rigidification is a sign of fear. We have seen this in our earlier examples, all of whom commit themselves to a rigid order, for fear of chaos.

The psychology of thought processes has shown that when we are afraid, we tend to 'stereotyped thinking'. Students are well acquainted with the phenomenon, but one can also experience it at a cocktail party or when meeting important people. Suddenly one finds oneself standing there with nothing to say, or only able to repeat the same prosaic phrases. It is as if our minds were in a rut or stuck in the groove of a cracked record. An even more extreme experience of this kind is the mental paralysis that manifests itself in complete absence of thought. One's mind goes blank. One cannot think of anything at all to say. This is being 'paralysed' with fear on the level of the mental faculties. We can, therefore, understand the physical stiffening and the mental retreat into extreme order as two aspects of the same phenomenon: the search for security in the face of fear. The underlying lack of security makes it impossible for the individual to retain a sense of flexibility. Flexibility means leaving an opening for chance, for the unpredictable. But when we are afraid we must, as we all know, try to reassure ourselves that we have everything under control. Whatever is unknown is unpredictable and, therefore, a threatening intrusion.

The keeping of order is a tool supporting the sense of being in control. This is evidently what Edith meant when she grasped for her formula 'order = sanity'. Schizophrenics faced with chaos generally grasp for order in the form of private logic. Their experience is so weird and incomprehensible that they must create their own, private ordering system. Thus paranoid fantasies, delusional systems, and strange interrelations between people, things, and events help them to bring order and meaning to what is happening within them. Often, the closer the crisis, the more extreme the order and the person's insistence on it. Sometimes, after the episode the person can recognize his 'thinking gone wild' as an effort to hold onto the real world.

But not all instances of private logic and order need be stamped as schizophrenic. In crises people often tend to seek support in unconventional ordering systems, or rather, unconventional ideologies which offer a sense of order and meaning. Some turn to far-out spiritual frames of reference. They may consult a fortune-teller or even a magnetopath when faced with a particularly difficult situation. I am thinking here of a woman who went to see a palm reader before deciding to give up her job. She wanted to be sure of making the 'right' decision and was afraid of taking too great a risk. The reassurance which she sought reflected her deep need – of finding the one and only right answer. She longed to find a kind of security we never can have. Similarly, we can understand people who join groups of spiritual tendencies, or follow a guru. The security which they are missing in just living according to their own values they reach out for in this other, unusual system. Often these groupings have strict orders with which one is obliged to comply; having to obey them provides a further grid to hold onto.

Some people invent their own systems, counting objects, performing ritualized actions when they are in distress. Obsessive–compulsive personalities regularly resort to such activities: they occupy themselves with counting and calculating for great stretches of time. Some tell of further, added emergency measures which they practise. When in special stress and in need of support, they count holes, cracks, or objects.

Depressive people also live in a world of their own private logic and order which is not immediately accessible to others. In Chapter 5 we shall examine in detail the case of Anne whose depressive order was tight and rigid, based on a private fantasy: that of hopelessness. Both hopelessness and guilt play a major role in depressive ordering systems. I am thinking in this context of an older woman whose husband had died three years before. Her family considered that this was an overly long time for mourning and suggested therapy. During the work we discovered a heavy sense of guilt towards her dead husband, for the woman had met a widower to whom she was attracted. Judging that it was not 'right', she withdrew from the world at large into a deep depression: guilt feelings predominated. The universe she constructed was private and isolated; but it gave her a certain sense of security, for it prevented her from getting further involved in her shameful and chaotic romantic stirrings.

Before leaving our example of 'order = sanity', it must be said here that not every tight timetable, however eccentric it may seem, is necessarily a sign of schizophrenic attempts at holding a world together. People whose lives are very busy can draw up schedules just as tight. By making note of their various appointments, they, too, are trying to avoid chaotic confusion. Generally speaking, ordering on paper, making a plan, can help in our conscious mastery of the world. Like map-making, keeping an agenda is a way of fixing points of orientation. It helps one to realize where one stands and how one might best proceed. And, in crises, a timetable can even closely resemble the one reproduced here. For example, during preparation for examinations, students may draw up very odd timetables. Similarly, young people who are growing up in quite ordinary circumstances often set up detailed schedules of what they want to do when; this helps them to find and stick to a personal sense of order, distinct from that of their surroundings. Common to all of these efforts at ordering time – the schizophrenic's, the businessman's, the student's, and the adolescent's – is their underlying striving for security through order. They are an attempt to get a grip on circumstances which the individual feels might get out of control or at least become uncomfortable. He feels the need to take the situation in hand.

Timetables, but also lists, charts, and tables can be the product of such doubts and fears. Think of the detailed lists of foodstuffs stored in bomb shelters in case of atomic war. These inventories of our well-stocked cellars help to comfort and reassure us in the face of chaos. The painting of a nineteenth-century American farm (Figure 3.3) derives from the same need: it is a pictorial inventory. Lining up – this time in images – in a neatly ordered fashion the property belonging to the farmer, grants him a sense of security and identity. Portraits have also been used for this purpose, for example, when the model is seen with all of the attributes of his trade and surrounded by representative elements of his world which show off his 'standing', his position, and his wealth.

Strict obedience to extreme ordering systems like the schizophrenic's timetable is practically impossible in normal states of mind. However, the young man in question most likely followed his schedule to perfection. The unhalting and undeviating compulsion to stick to an extreme order – he is obsessed by it – is quite typical of such states. There is no room for compromise: the order is too important as an anchor in sanity to be neglected. We can think here of Edith whose self-constructed *Ersatz* reality became so much more important than the real world. Obeying its dictates and conforming to its order can easily take precedence over complying with the demands of the outside world.

The other side of the coin of keeping order is its positive and strengthening aspects. Making a plan and following it can, in fact, be a very satisfying and ego-strengthening act. It does activate energy and works against regressive impulses. Directed activity in the outside world, especially creating and following order, can help to further a person's sense of identity, constancy, development, and accomplishment. It belongs to the process of strengthening the ego. And that is an essential aspect of every development.

In conclusion we can say that all three of the people in the face of chaos whom we have met in this chapter sacrifice their basic human flexibility in favour of order. But the order which they create leaves no room for chaos. It is characterized by harmony and peace, security and control. Significant is the underlying need which such ordering evidently fulfils: a need for security in the face of danger. And this, too, was apparent in all of our examples: the need to retreat from a reality which was experienced as threatening.

The element of retreat is not to be under-estimated. Retreat, standing back, taking one's emotional distance, and looking at something from a critical distance all belong together as typically human capacities. In our examples, the movement was too extreme:

Figure 3.3 Edward Hicks, The Cornell Farm (1848), National Gallery of Art, Washington DC

it drew the people so far away from life that no return was possible. Even more extreme examples exist: people who, for example, avoid contact with certain objects, which they consider dirty, infectious, or in some way harmful. From insects to water taps, from electricity to dust, the list of possible 'phobias' is long. For some, the fear of being touched is especially constellated by people. They therefore avoid physical contact, refusing even to shake hands or just shying away from people. Nevertheless, generally speaking, the need for retreat and withdrawal is a valid need. But it requires its complement in being able to approach, to go towards, to contact, and to get involved emotionally and physically. We need to be able to enter into contact with people, things, and events, to register and to be moved by the direct impressions of life around us. Without a combination of these two basic and complementary movements, we are sadly impoverished. In Chapter 5 we shall discuss in more detail the necessary complementarity of the need for direct impressions from close-up and the need to withdraw and distance oneself.

The people described in this chapter all isolated themselves in a world of their own from which escape became impossible. With-drawing from chaotic circumstances may have offered them the promise of avoiding suffering, but it also contributed to widening the gap between dream and reality. The haven of dream-world order was so soothing as to prevent any further communication with the mainland of life's turmoils. And the greater the gap between these two worlds, the more difficult it is to bridge and to bear. Opting for order and fantasy meant rejecting chaos and reality.

Whereas, for these people order and chaos appear as two extreme opposites, natural science is evolving a model of order and chaos which is integrative. All of our three examples tended to create and hold on to an extremely rigid and unpliable image of order. In it many elements of life had no place. Chaos was excluded, and many aspects of normal life – conflict, strife, emotions – went under the name of chaos and were consequently rejected. In nature, as scientists are presently discovering, chaos and order are not irreconcilable opposites. Chaos appears rather as a step on the way from one order to the next. It reveals itself as an indispensable aspect of development and growth. These and other observations on the characteristics of chaos and order in nature will be the subject of the next chapter.

Chapter 4

Modern science's views on chaos and order and what they imply for man

Scientific investigation in the past concentrated its attention on the discovery of the laws which apparently rule our universe. Scientists sought and found many predictable elements in nature; they found order and regularity. And when they did accidentally come upon chaos, they spontaneously rejected it as too bizarre. Such was the case of the French mathematician Henri Poincaré in 1889 (Breuer 1985: 47).

In the last twenty years, however, science has raised chaos to a respectable object of investigation. Its phenomenology and its dynamics are presently being studied by physicists, physicians, mathematicians, chemists, biologists, and computer scientists. All of these fields are engaged in what today goes under the name of 'chaos research'.

How are we to understand this intense interest in chaos? On the one hand, the computer is responsible. With its extraordinary capacity for complex and rapid calculations, it provides an excellent tool for the study of chaos. Seemingly chaotic data can be plotted so as to reveal their hidden correspondences: from what appears as a jumble of disparate information, patterns emerge. Without the help of the computer, chaos research as it is being practised today, would be practically impossible.

On the other hand, the awakening of scientific curiosity in the domain of chaos can be interpreted as a manifestation of the collective unconscious at work. Compensating for the dominant ideas and values in our society, the collective unconscious is stirring up that which has been rejected. Our contemporary exaggeration of the value of order would, therefore, automatically be calling forth an upsurge of interest in the opposite, chaos. From this point of view, modern science is fulfilling the same function and playing the same role as the folk customs and beliefs of earlier ages. That is, it is helping the individual and the group to accept and integrate chaos as a fact of life. One may readily say that today more than ever in the history of mankind, chaos belongs to our world picture. For science has come to see our world as being in a state of constant movement, change, and growth. Nothing is static and stable, neither the planets nor the continents, neither small organic organisms nor the human body itself. Within such a universe chaos plays a major role. It is an integral part of natural order and in itself is not entirely without order.

So we see that science has come to reconcile chaos and order. The two terms no longer appear as mutually exclusive. They can and do coexist in the life processes of natural organisms. In this chapter these recent scientific discoveries will be surveyed. Of fundamental interest here is their eventual applicability to humanity. Therefore, after first presenting the theories on chaos and order which seem pertinent, I shall go on to suggest what they might look like in the realm of human experience. It is helpful to sum up the discoveries in a few succinct points:

1 Chaos can reveal order: *patterns* and *scenarios* (*order in chaos*).
2 Order can emerge from chaos in the following way (*order from chaos*).
3 Component parts of a system co-operate to find order (*synergetics*).
4 This can happen when a certain *critical point* is reached.
5 Then the system becomes *unstable*.
6 *Non-linearity* governs these transformative processes.
7 The *time factor* is important.
8 Development can take place in sudden leaps (*saltation*) or gradually.
9 In extremely unstable conditions, slight changes can provoke major, unpredictable effects (*the butterfly principle*).
10 *Sensitivity* and *flexibility* are key traits in the survival of natural organisms.

THE SCIENTIFIC PRINCIPLES

Order in chaos

Scientists have found that chaos can reveal a certain order, although it may not be immediately apparent. One must find the right perspective to be able to perceive this orderliness. Sometimes it can be observed under a microscope, with the help of computer calculations, or even by making much simpler changes in perspective. For example, seemingly chaotic cloud formations reveal their structuredness when seen from the perspective of a satellite. Formations of water, land, even cities can be seen in their orderliness when the angle is changed. Think of the very banal example of a city seen from a church tower or the sight of land or water formations offered from the window of an airplane flying above them. Furthermore, science has determined that all turbulences – whether they are caused by a spoon stirring cream into coffee or by the streaming of masses of gasses, air, water, or any other liquid – share certain basic similarities: shapes and patterns which resemble each other can be observed. Another perspective enabling us to discern order in chaos is time: its passage permits us to see things in a new way. And so, we sleep on a problem, having come to learn that after laying it thus to rest, we can see it with greater clarity. Chaos can reveal a certain order: our problem is finding the proper perspective to be able to perceive it.

In the same vein we can understand the new perspectives which the computer offers us for discovering the order inherent in chaos. Scientists have come to find, for example, that chaotic events such as earthquakes which seem to erupt completely unexpectedly (in a chaotic fashion and wreaking chaos) occur with a certain predictable regularity. Charting their occurrence reveals patterns that point to the presence of unstable earth masses underlying the areas in question. In this way, future quakes can be predicted.

Computers have also made feasible and practicable certain extremely complex mathematical calculations which reveal the various ways systems pass from an ordered original state into a chaotic one: 'paths into chaos' have been charted. They are called 'chaos scenarios' and are known by the names of their discoverers. The three most famous are the Feigenbaum scenario, the Pomeau–Manneville scenario, and the Ruelle–Takens scenario. The most diverse phenomena follow these paths, for example, the

Bénard cells described later can be brought to a chaotic cooking point through the Feigenbaum scenario, and the transition from a regular heartbeat to a fluttering murmur follows the same path. (The physics experiment with the Taylor cells and the chemical experiment known as the Belousov–Zhabotinski reaction both follow the Ruelle–Takens scenario on their way into chaos.)

The term 'deterministic chaos' has been coined to describe seemingly disordered states which, however, reveal a certain degree of order. It is used to apply to a specific type of disorder which is in part predictable and shows certain regularities; furthermore, it can be defined by a limited number of variables.

Needless to say, not all chaos is 'deterministic chaos'. For example, the disordered activity which one observes in spaghetti sauce brought to a boil is not deterministic. Its disorder is stochastic and is so irregular that it cannot be described by a limited number of variables. It is chaos but not 'deterministic' chaos.

Order from chaos

The discovery of this principle is one of the earliest in chaos research. It is due to the 1977 Nobel prize winner, Ilya Prigogine. This theoretical physicist observed the phenomenon in thermo-dynamic systems in far from equilibrium states. He saw how the basic instability of such systems (like the Bénard convection cells discussed below) enabled them to adapt readily to changed conditions. The component molecules can thus evolve from chaos to order according to the principle of self-organization outlined below.

Synergetics

Since Ilya Prigogine's discoveries, scientists from various fields have discovered other systems which pass from one stage of order through a chaotic or disordered phase to arrive at a new and more complex stage of order. This order is better adapted to the altered situation at hand. The phenomenon, known as 'self-organization', or 'synergetics', has been found to apply to physics, chemistry, biology, mathematics, sociology, and ecology.

One of the most comprehensible experiments showing synergetics at work has been described by the Zurich physics professor, Ernst Brun (1985). A pan with alu powder and silicone oil is heated. When the temperature reaches a certain point, a seemingly disordered activity begins to take place. Completely irregular cells (see Figure 4.1a) form: this is convection at work. The cells circulate in a random manner; they transform in size and shape. After a while, they take on more uniform size and shape. Finally they gather together into a coherent structure, the honeycomb shape (see Figure 4.1b).

The Bénard convection cells, as they are called, adapt to the rise in temperature by a process of transformation. As the oil is heated, it becomes unstable. The newly formed cells adapt to the altered conditions by co-operating together. They ultimately find a new and more complex order through their co-operative behaviour.

This reaction, which is typical of such thermodynamic systems in far from equilibrium states, is a common phenomenon in the world around us. It can be observed in cloud formations as well as in basalt pillars and dried-up lake beds. It is, however, important to note that not all fluids to which heat is thus applied react in this way: tomato sauce, for example, when exposed to such a rise in temperature, does not evolve from chaos to order: it persists in a completely disordered, chaotic bubbling of irregular cells. And, as we noted above, when the Bénard cells themselves are further heated they proceed into chaos (along the path known as the Feigenbaum scenario).

This experiment nicely demonstrates the phenomenon described by Ilya Prigogine, who also referred to thermodynamic systems in far from equilibrium states. Many other experiments demonstrate the same properties. I choose here to present Hermann Haken's (1978) work with the laser. For Haken – an experimental physicist (Prigogine is a theoretical physicist) to whom this discovery is sometimes attributed – observed it in the laser and gave the name 'synergetics' to the self-organizing processes which he observed. Hermann Haken found that when laser atoms are stimulated by a weak source of energy, they oscillate slowly and in a completely uncoordinated or random (chaotic) manner. They then bring forth a light which is no different from normal lamp light. When, however, a more intense current is applied to the same atoms, they produce the characteristic thin and powerful light which we know as the laser. They do so by oscillating together in a very uniform and rapid manner. The co-operative activity of the component atoms is an automatic reaction to the intensified current.

Ilya Prigogine (Prigogine and Stengers 1984) described this

Figure 4.1   Bénard cells
Source: Brun (1986)

phenomenon in anthropomorphic terms which are especially enlightening for our purposes. He called the molecules he studied 'hypnons' and said that they are like sleepwalkers: when they sense a change in conditions, they awake and begin communicating together in order to find a new order, better adapted to the situation at hand. They go from random, disordered activity in which each 'sleepwalks' on its own to uniform, co-operative behaviour. From their chaotic state arises order, and this is thanks to their communication with each other.

We shall now take a more detailed look at the way in which this transformative process from chaos to order evolves.

Critical points

The laser atoms readapt in a completely different manner, finding their characteristic laser beam light when their source of energy reaches a certain intensity – a critical point. In the Bénard cells, raising their temperature to a specific degree provokes their co-ordinated readaptation. In other systems, similar critical points must be reached before any such co-operative reorganization can occur. It is as if the parts of a system sense that 'the heat is on' – the temperature rises, the energy becomes intensified – and then feel the urgency of finding a mutually satisfying manner of reacting together, as a unit, to the new situation.

At such a critical point, a system can find new order. Other critical points exist at which a system can go from order to chaos. Essential in the critical points principle is the point at which transformation takes place.

Instability

In order for change to be effected, the system must become destabilized. In the laser, the component atoms become destabilized through an increase in the energy source which stimulates them. The Bénard cells, which rather tend to instability, become more unstable and mobile when the temperature they are exposed to is raised. Openness to the surrounding conditions characterizes all of the non-linear systems studied (even the healthy human body): this makes them basically unstable and potentially adaptable. In contrast, systems characterized by stability are less open to the environment and less capable of adaptation.

Non-linearity

The thermodynamic systems to which Ilya Prigogine refers are all non-linear systems. That is, their sum is more than the total of their parts. Change, therefore, takes place within them in a non-linear fashion, according to a 'summation effect', e.g. raising the temperature merely one degree can trigger a major effect. Effects are then disproportionate to their causes. In such systems, complicated feedback mechanisms are at play: simple laws of cause and effect do not suffice to explain the changes one observes. Non-linearity is an essential trait of all of the systems studied; it applies to natural organisms (and humanity) as well.

The time factor

Scientists assert the all-importance of the time factor in being able to observe such processes. The evolution of order out of chaos (the self-organizing processes described above) can take a very long time to manifest. Extreme patience is demanded of the scientists waiting to see how the systems arrive at their new order. Professor Brun (1985) stresses this point as he describes what happens when one destroys the honeycomb shape of the Bénard cells by stirring the solution. After a short while, the irregular cells reappear. Then follows a slow phase of adaptation at the end of which the honeycomb structure reappears.

> Order requires time and patience; for the attentive observer it is not lost time. Following this fascinating phase over the space of many minutes is worthwhile. The development and disappearance of the convection cells as they try to find their optimal, regular form is one of the most impressive examples of what such a simple experiment can offer.
>
> (Brun 1985: 292)

Saltation

When transformation does finally take place, it may appear rather suddenly. Then the saltation principle is at work. In the past few years macroevolutionists have suggested that this principle determines evolutionary processes in nature. The theory, which is not new, was presented anew in 1972 by Miles Eldredge and Stephen Gould (in Taylor 1983: 16–17). According to them, not all evolutionary change took place gradually, as Darwin had proposed. Actually, these two scientists suggested that change was not the result of a slow process of adaptation to ever-changing conditions. Instead, they felt that it took place suddenly in chaotic leaps.

Since then, macroevolutionists rather imagine that a combination of these two forces – the slow and gradual transformative forces and the sudden and chaotic leaps – determined evolution.

The saltation principle of evolution would be stating something like the following. At critical points, when change is necessary and difficult to achieve, cells can reorganize all of a sudden. They would then go through the process described above, traversing chaos to find a new and ultimately better suited order. Distinctive in this view of evolution is the rapidity of the change and the place granted to chaos as a step in the evolutionary processes.

André Sakharov suggested in 1966 that matter on earth was formed in just such a moment (see Prigogine and Stengers, 1984: 230). A far from equilibrium state had been reached. The unstable system, capable of major change at the drop of a hat, pin – or at the batting of a butterfly's wings – made a sudden leap through a chaotic state into a new state of order. That leap was the beginning of the earth as we know it.

The butterfly principle

According to the butterfly principle, major unpredictable changes can occur – chaotic conditions arise – when a situation is slightly altered. Edward N. Lorenz is the meteorologist who discovered this principle while studying weather patterns (quoted in Breuer 1985: 50). He found that his computer calculations of the weather changed drastically if he fed the computer slightly different data. And he concluded that in some situations, minor variations in initial conditions can lead to unpredictable results: the vibrations of a butterfly flapping its wings could make things look entirely different from what is expected. Calculating such changes is hardly possible: they are, therefore, unpredictable and chaotic. This principle is observed in particularly unstable situations, like weather conditions. Extreme instability sets the stage for the sudden and surprising emergence of the butterfly principle. One may also formulate this principle in the following terms: under extreme conditions, minimal causes provoke extreme and unforeseeable results.

Sensitivity and flexibility

Basic to all of these principles is the sensitivity of the systems studied. Original observations on such behaviour were made on thermodynamic systems in far from equilibrium states. As we have seen, they are by definition open systems and so unstable as to be able to react readily to changes in their environment. In this respect they must be contrasted to systems in equilibrium, which tend to stability and remain inert, static, and inflexible when changes in their milieu occur.

Paul Weiss is a theoretical and experimental biologist who clearly affirms that natural organisms are uniquely sensitive to their milieu and are, consequently, involved in a constant exchange of matter and energy with their surroundings (Weiss 1973). This means that they are in a continual process of ordering and re-ordering, adapting and re-adapting to changes that occur in their outer and inner worlds.

Furthermore, Weiss states that an organism that is to survive requires just such sensitivity, for it must be able to sense the need for new adaptations. With other biologists, he speaks of the all-importance not of adaptation but of flexibility. Flexibility is the ultimate test of strength in the fight for survival. An inflexible organism may be able to hold its own in an antiquated structure, but as soon as a new adaptation is required, it will crack under the force of events. Gordon Rattray Taylor, a scientific journalist, cites the example of animals who have adapted so as to be able to devour a certain type of prey (Taylor 1983). When they have eaten up all of the members of the species, they must be able to re-adapt once again or else they will starve and die out. Or, as Taylor suggests, it is not difficult to put on a spacesuit in order to adapt to outer space. The trick is to be able to take it off again.

APPLICATIONS TO HUMANITY

Although our interest is in the applicability of the above-mentioned ideas to the human psyche, we cannot neglect to mention here, if only briefly, their applicability to the human body. Very recent scientific research, as we have hinted earlier, is discovering basic resemblances between the physiological human system and the far from equilibrium systems described above. Composed of 70 per cent water, the human body is open to change and in a continual process of exchange of matter and energy with its surroundings. It is, therefore, marked by a basic instability, and hence, a capacity for sensing and adapting to alterations in its milieu. Seen from this perspective, chaos appears to be a natural, even necessary aspect of the normal human body. Rigid order characterizes sickness. Studies in medical centres throughout the world – of brain activity, heartbeat, metabolism, and cell growth – all seem to be verifying this hypothesis. Electroencephalograms of epileptics during a seizure show very regular, ordered curves; normal encephalograms show more irregularities and change. Normal heartbeats seen on an electrocardiogram reveal periodic changes which can vary from second to second. A sick heart shows less flexibility; its rhythms can be very regular and orderly, or they can develop an irregularity from which they can recover only with great difficulty. A metabolism functioning properly is a system of ordered chaos; too much harmony and order is a sure sign that something is wrong. Also, leukaemia patients have a white blood count that fluctuates between two extremes; in healthy people there is a great deal more fluctuation – chaos – in the cell count. Tumour cells grow according to definite laws, regardless of any outer change; medication or other treatments have little or no effect on their growth. Healthy cells are continually adapting to changes in their milieu by producing hormones. We might add here that the AIDS virus destroys the sensitivity and flexibility of the immune system, a system which is renowned for its unique adaptability. It is in a constant state of flux as it fights off infections which enter the body.

All of this research, which is still very new and controversial, indicates that the healthy human body goes through periods of chaotic instability in order to adapt to new and altered situations in an appropriate manner. Sensitivity and flexibility characterize its functioning. In the light of these findings chaos appears, as in other organic (but also inorganic) organisms, as a necessary adjustment phase, allowing change to take place: it is essential for health and for life itself.

Change is one of the most exciting but also most frightening phenomena in life. If, in fact, change takes place via an excursion into chaos, then it is an inevitable reality of living organisms. Chaos as a step on the way to new order, instability as a necessary prerequisite to change – these are completely different ways of evaluating what we have come to understand as archetypally frightening realities. They are as revolutionary for modern man as the idea that chaos can be in part determined, predicted, and has an order of its own. And yet, we are closing the loop to the ancient image of a fruitful chaos. Yes, chaos can be fruitful – for its capacity of allowing new order to emerge.

Order in chaos

The idea of chaos having a certain order is fascinating when applied to humanity. As we saw in the scientific discoveries, the order behind chaos becomes apparent through taking up a new perspective. If we can find the right perspective, we can see the order underlying what at first sight seems to be pure chaos. This is definitely the case in our psychological experience of chaos. As soon as we find the proper critical distance, we are able to distinguish elements of chaos and even underlying 'psycho-logical' patterns and mechanisms. This makes our chaos in part 'deterministic' and predictable; although one cannot pretend that it is entirely predictable nor that it can be described by a limited number of variables. Humanity and human nature are characterized by an unlimited number of variables. That is why computers cannot duplicate us. Nevertheless, by applying our attention to chaos, we can, with much time and effort, discover a certain order underlying it.

In psychotherapy we apply ourselves to discerning the patterns of each individual's chaos. This helps to render it less threatening, more acceptable and comprehensible. Understanding what triggered it, why it erupted at just that moment and what it means are all aspects of the therapeutic search for order in chaos. During our investigations, we inevitably come upon specific patterns. They are all *typically human 'paths into chaos'*, for they are naturally provoked by situations and events to which every human being is exposed in the course of a lifetime. They may be due to the *biological facts of life*. In this category of *chaos scenarios* we can place the crises known to arise in the typical transition phases, in puberty, mid-life, menopause, old age. At these times we need to find a new adaptation, for our life conditions are changing. The more difficult it is to arrive at the appropriate change in attitude and lifestyle, the greater our stress factor. The stage is set for a chaotic crisis in which, as we shall see, psyche, soma, and milieu interact to press for the necessary readaptation. Under the heading 'synergetics' we shall examine a typical 'old age chaos scenario'.

Other typical situations which are liable to provoke chaos have
to do with the *psychological and social facts of life*: when we experience
a disappointment in love or in our career; when we are faced with
separation from a loved one, be it through death, divorce, or even
leaving home; when we sense a conflict between our own needs
and those of our milieu. All of these occasions can easily lead to
the eruption of chaos in the life of the individual.

I could cite as examples any one of the many cases of people
with whom I have worked. Let us take that of a woman whose
panic attacks were, from her perspective, absolutely unexpected
and incomprehensible. They were, accordingly, frightening for
her. She is happy with her husband and three children. She has
everything she wants. She is busy with pleasant activities: taking
care of the children and the household. She has friends with whom
she feels comfortable. She gets along well with her parents as well
as with her brothers and sisters. Everything should be fine. There
is no reason for panic attacks. And from her perspective this is true:
she feels strongly that nothing at all is lacking or amiss. This chaotic
eruption of panic in a seemingly satisfying life is superfluous,
ridiculous, incomprehensible, and utterly unacceptable. However,
by concentrating on the attacks themselves, we discover certain
repetitive patterns. They invariably occur on specific occasions,
like when she sends the children off to school, or when she and
her husband go away on vacation together alone. Unconsciously,
without her being aware of it, the woman is reacting to situations
of separation. Her chaos is determined by her difficulty in dealing
with separations. The more the pattern becomes evident, the more
she can recall other, similar types of circumstances in which she has
reacted in an unexpectedly intense manner: when she had to go to
school herself, when she left home for camp, and also when she
married and left her family definitively. As our work progresses,
we slowly discover the way in which her fear of separation arose.
It had its roots in early childhood and reached its peak now when
she had a family of her own.

Through our introspective work, the woman becomes able to
comprehend her chaos. Its eruption in her life feels less surprising.
She learns to face her fears, to express them, and to understand
them instead of blocking them off and pretending they do not
exist. In this way, she comes to realize, for example, that she
feels extremely dependent and gradually learns to acquire more
autonomy. She begins to do things on her own, from getting

a part-time job to going away for a few days alone, to making decisions without consulting with all of her friends beforehand. She, thus, gets the feeling that she could, if need be, manage on her own: her fears of being left alone – of separation – are greatly reduced. Basic to such a development is the recognition of the patterns, the recurring behaviour patterns which belong to oneself and which elucidate one's own, personal path into chaos.

From chaos order can emerge

All endeavours in psychotherapy are based on this principle. It presupposes the capacity for letting chaos be and allowing it to lead one to a new order. In accord with our previous observations from the models of the collective unconscious, this means that chaos is accepted and examined as a potentially valuable experience. And so we can clearly affirm that on the level of humanity, from chaos order can emerge, providing that we do not block chaos by defending against it and/or taking medication to suppress it. That is not to say that medication should never be taken. But the open encounter with chaos requires a certain degree of commitment to facing and unravelling the forces at work.

Chapter 5 is devoted to a detailed description of ways in which we try to stimulate the capacity for getting involved in chaos through psychotherapy. In general terms, we can say that we encourage the direct, emotional experience of chaos, for it is the essential prerequisite for any self-organizing processes.

I can cite here the example of a young man who was studying to become a high school teacher. He was in the midst of his practical training when he found himself overcome with such fear that he stayed home for the next few days. He consulted me as he was distraught and did not know how he could possibly continue. There was no doubt in his mind that he had chosen the right profession: all he had to do was to get over this fear. As the man was not aware of any grounds for his fears and sensed no underlying conflicts in relation to teaching, I felt that we had to try to discover what his fear was all about. I suggested that we try to get involved with it once again, and thus attempt to find out what it had to say and where it might be leading him. The man agreed, although he did not relish the prospect. We spent two consecutive hours retrieving the moment of dread and then discussing it. By contacting his feelings of fear, the physical sensations associated with them and remaining open to images, associations, and memories that emerged, we discovered that the man had extraordinary fears of exposure. He could not really imagine standing up in front of a class all of his life. He had actually chosen the profession on the prompting of a good friend who felt he would make an excellent teacher. On further reflection, based on what we had found out, the 'teacher-to-be' decided that it was preferable for him to learn another profession rather than to expose himself to such fears for the next forty years of his life. He had no desire to go on to discover why he had such fears of exposure, nor why he should have been so influenced by his friend. But he did sense that some new order was needed. From his chaotic experience, order emerged. Within a few short weeks the young man found a job which looked interesting. He started right away and soon came to feel that this was what he was 'meant to do', as he said. This was the kind of work he was really suited to. The chaotic fears that he had experienced had been a shrill alarm signal pointing to his need for another, hitherto unimaginable, kind of order.

Self-organization through communication – synergetics

At the moment when the system senses the need for change, seemingly chaotic activity begins. It has been postulated that at this time the cells are communicating to find together a common solution to the problem at hand: how to adapt in an optimal way. This principle is especially striking when applied to humanity. If we understand ourselves as a psycho-somatico-social whole, then these aspects of our being can be considered as the component elements of our system. At critical times they begin communicating together in order to reach a new type of order better suited to the demands of the moment.

And, in fact, this is what we observe. How often do we find the body reacting, speaking up in a loud voice, and announcing new needs? Or an inexplicable state of mind announces itself and demands to be heard in dreams, obsessive thoughts, intense emotional reactions. And, not infrequently, a prodding from our milieu, from our partner, for example, or even an event in the outside world helps us to become aware that it is time for change. All of these diverse bits of information are filtered into the system; each has its bit to communicate. Each plays its part in pressing for change. It is as if all were intent on creating a turmoil, forcing us to realize that our critical point has been reached and that we need to find a new and more appropriate order.

In such moments we are under special stress. Things can easily seem chaotic. Various voices – most often irreconcilable with each other and especially with the former order – make themselves heard. If the confusion can be accepted and differentiated, new order can arise relatively easily. Frequently, however, we tend to block off these perceptions. We try to ignore what we sense is going on inside, pushing the thoughts and feelings away (with will power or tranquillizers), trivializing the physical pain or silencing it with medication. And we often also withdraw from our milieu, refusing any deeper forms of communication with it. In Chapter 3 we saw what such withdrawal and suppression of communication with the inner and outer world can look like. These defensive measures are meant to stop the process which has begun. We avoid entering into the chaotic communication for fear of change: we hold fast to the old order and do our utmost to avoid being forced to reappraise our situation.

For example, we can suddenly realize that we have difficulty in driving the car. Beset with fantasies of terrifying accidents, we have trouble concentrating our attention on the road. The disturbance can become so bothersome that we begin to reflect on what may lie at the bottom of it: some unconscious conflict must be getting in the way of our 'normal' functioning in reality. If we do not at this time begin to reflect and face the problem, then other elements may go on to prompt us. We may develop an unusually fast pulse or particularly heavy perspiration. If we are still not able to examine our situation, perhaps family or friends begin to pressure us to do something about it, or strange accidents can even occur. The ways in which our psycho-somatic-social system reacts and interacts are innumerable and complex.

Interesting for us is the idea of the automatic interaction of these three aspects of being in order to find a new and better suited adaptation. Such a model helps to explain the fact that physical reactions play an important role in psychic disturbances. They are frequently accompanying symptoms. And, as family therapists have noted for some time, the milieu also has its part to play in the development of psychological and somatic disorders.

In the following example, a change in the person's milieu led him to a chaotic crisis. He could not imagine finding a new order and considered ending his life, for the old order no longer worked.

This type of dead-end rigidification is a common problem for the aged in modern industrial societies. A 67-year-old man, widowed for the past twenty years, had managed quite well on his own: he worked and saw a group of friends regularly. He cooked and washed for himself and went to see his only daughter for a few days every month. After retirement he was able to continue working part time. Then, one day, he was laid off. The man became depressed and had thoughts of suicide. While telephoning her father around this time, his daughter noticed that something was wrong. She went to see him and brought him back to her home. But he just sat around and, when spoken to, wallowed in negative thoughts. After a while his daughter decided to send him to see a therapist. He was given medication for his depression and during his weekly sessions talked about his impossible situation. With time he came to realize how important his independence was for him. The thought of no longer being able to work and perhaps of needing his daughter's help was unacceptable. For him, living meant living alone and depending on no one. The communication which had taken place within him had manifested first in his psychological symptoms: a depressive reaction. This psychological symptom did not enable the man to readapt immediately. Finding new order in old age can seem like an insurmountable problem. But, finally, the man's daughter, sensing that he was at a dead-end, pressed for change. Through this prodding from his milieu (social aspect) a readaptation became feasible. Medication (somatic aspect) for his depression (psychological aspect) helped the man to confront his problems in therapy (psychological approach). Here his inner conflict could be raised to consciousness. At the end of several months' work in therapy, the man came to the following, for him acceptable decision. He would live with his daughter and would help her by doing the gardening: in this way his need for independence could be satisfied to a certain degree, but in a manner which was realistic and better suited to the actual circumstances of his life.

Critical points

The scientific theory states that change takes place at certain critical points, for example, when the heat applied to a system reaches a critical temperature. The same may well be true of individuals: change occurs when the need becomes pressing. When the heat is raised, when things get too hot, when something must happen to ensure adequate adaptation to new conditions, at such moments change becomes an unavoidable necessity. In fact, significant changes can most likely only take place when the individual senses their urgency.

But, of course, the stress factor (as we can call the raised heat in human terms) varies from person to person. In some people, the basic sensitivity is such that the need for change is sensed earlier than in others; that is, their critical point is lower or they perceive it sooner. It can make itself felt more readily and, if we can work with it consciously, the necessary re-adaptation can be effected under less extreme pressure. Of basic importance is sensing when this point has been reached and being able to face the need for change and to reflect on it. A main goal of psychotherapy is increasing sensitivity to one's critical points and the capacity to reflect on them. In this manner, they can be acted on more spontaneously and, therefore, under less painfully extreme conditions.

A businessman sought therapy when such a critical point in his life had been reached: he had a nervous collapse one day. It had been prompted by several factors which, in combination, had raised his stress beyond a tolerable degree. He had been working for a few years in a very demanding and prestigious job under difficult conditions. The firm was being restructured and there was a great deal of tension at work. Around the time of the collapse he had been making plans for a long-desired and costly vacation. His wife was pregnant with her first child; they were thinking of building a house and had just found a suitable, but overly expensive site. The man turned forty and around the same time, his tax returns were due. All of these various factors contributed to making his situation untenable. Evidently 'the heat was on'. One may well wonder why he did not sense it earlier, for example, in his overly stressful job situation. His relative insensitivity to his critical point was due to an extraordinary need for achievement. It had developed as a result of a difficult (and repressed) childhood when he had suffered much under repeated failures and deceptions. I shall return to this background and the complex mechanisms which were at work here in the section on non-linearity (pp. 88–9).

A woman under similar strain in her very responsible position, did not react in such an abrupt manner but, through the years, developed ulcers which were, accordingly, treated. Her system's warning of the critical point had not been understood as a valuable signal indicating the necessity of re-evaluating her lifestyle. Only many years after the onset of the ulcers did she realize the importance of re-examining the way she was living: when her husband threatened to leave her. At this time, she felt the heat on: she sensed that something must be wrong and felt her desperation: chaos erupted and enabled her to begin the search for a new order.

A 50-year-old man, a top manager, had a serious heart attack when he was granted the position which he had hoped for throughout his career. The pressure under which he had worked until then had been great, but the man never paid attention to the various symptoms, alarm signals which had made themselves felt before. And so, he had gone through periods of sleeplessness and over-excitement which he had learned to silence, taking sleeping pills and regularly drinking large quantities of alcohol when he came home from work. He needed relaxation; he needed to reduce the pressures he was feeling. He did so with the help of pills and alcohol, as well as with physical exercise. His methods, however, failed him when the new job offer came up: his critical point had been reached. Then, a new order was prescribed for him. His medical doctors demanded complete rest for a long period; they suggested that he not take the new job: it would be too much for him. What he needed most of all, in their opinion, was a low stress, comfortable job. That was what they judged that his body could cope with. For the man, this meant living according to quite different principles, putting his body and its needs first. The prescription was difficult to fill, for the order it implied had been quite inconceivable for the man until this point.

Non-linearity

The three-dimensional model (psycho-somatico-social) described above shows the complexity of the interactions which motivate human behaviour. They cannot be explained by simple cause and effect mechanisms. Such an idea is often difficult for people to understand. They want to find the direct cause (one and only) for a state of mind and, after once finding it, they expect the negative effects to disappear immediately. This is a mechanistic model which may well apply to machines, but it does not suffice to explain the self-organizing processes which scientists observe both in physical and chemical events and in nature.

The complex feedback mechanisms at work in men and women

are difficult to understand: here reigns not logic but 'psycho-logic' (which is non-linear). That is not to say that the psychological mechanisms cannot be understood at all. But it is difficult to understand them. Perhaps we can only really grasp a very small portion of what goes on inside ourselves. The indispensable prerequisite for any and all understanding is that attention should be focused on oneself: on one's psychological state, one's physical state, and one's social interactions.

When we think back to the first example sketched in the section on critical points (p. 86), this complexity is clearly visible. The man in question had trouble understanding that he could have had a nervous collapse at this time. When he tried to reconstruct what had happened to him, he came upon the tax returns, but such a minor thing did not seem a sufficient cause to explain the breakdown. In fact, it was not sufficient. But we were in the presence of a summation effect. As we saw, many factors in the man's actual situation compounded to provoke his intense reaction. Furthermore, many as yet unconscious realities were at work here. It took time to unravel the various threads and discover the complex mechanisms underlying the apparently inexplicable breakdown. The man's intensely achievement-oriented lifestyle had 'psycho-logical' ramifications, which he could not easily discern nor accept, for they were unconscious and seemed illogical. Why should he want somehow not to please his wife and his boss? In other words, why should something in him be intent on experiencing failure? His need to be able to fail, to reveal finally his incapacity and still to meet with understanding and concern was great. It had never been fufilled before. These psychological mechanisms had a logic of their own in which factors of which the man had not been aware until now had to be unearthed and considered.

The time factor

The process of raising the level of self-awareness is necessarily time consuming. Similarly, it may and often does take a long time before one can observe any change, any evolution of new order. Time is an unavoidable necessity when working with such complex systems as those described above – including the natural organism, man. A psychotherapist needs the same patience as the physicist who must sit and wait through long periods of seeming inactivity before he can see the spontaneous emergence of order which he suspects will take place. Naturally, the people involved in such a process also need patience, perhaps more than the therapist, for they often do not possess the assurance that new order can be found.

Psychotherapy is necessarily a time-consuming process: it takes longer than one would generally like for a new and better suited adaptation to establish itself. This is because the old order and its patterns are deeply entrenched: they have been practised for many years and the motivations underlying them are unconscious. We normally tend to act in a somewhat automatic way, without realizing how and why we do so.

A woman sought therapy because of an eating disorder: her eating and vomiting patterns had developed during puberty. Now that she was married, she was ashamed of her long-standing habit. After several years of intensive psychotherapy, the symptoms that plagued her disappeared. The process was gradual. Slowly we saw how her attitude towards food, towards herself as a woman, and towards her body and its appearance changed. She came to be aware of the fact that her forced eating and vomiting habits were an important way in which she tried to resolve inner pressures. As this behaviour pattern was very remote from her conscious mind, it took a long time for her to be able to recognize and accept these psychological facts of her being. Nor was it easy for her to learn to perceive and meet the pressure she felt in a more direct and adequate manner. But, as her recognition grew, a new order slowly became established. At the end of our work, she had come to understand her old behaviour pattern and what it involved. And she was freed from it.

Saltation

That human development can take place in leaps and bounds is no surprise for us. We are accustomed to seeing, for example, how a child at school drags on with an inappropriate attitude: he seems immature, has not yet developed a satisfying way of being with other children: he has not quite found himself. It is as if he were retarded in his development. Then, suddenly and without warning, 'the penny drops', as the saying goes. With no previous signs that a change was in the offing, a new adaptation is suddenly there. The process is chaotic and unpredictable. Similar 'jumps' take place later on in life, under the stress of circumstances. A woman who obediently followed her role model and remained a passive, seemingly unreflective wife suddenly becomes an independent and vivaciously enterprising widow.

Other sudden leaps may more clearly bear the seal of chaos. In the development of infants we witness stages which seem to be without rhyme or reason. We perceive no order, no regularity, nothing in the way of a visible pattern for a certain time. But then, suddenly, the apparently unmotivated crying and discontent stop and we realize that the child has reached another stage: it has just taken a chaotic developmental leap, passing from one level to another via a chaotic transition phase.

In the course of psychotherapy we witness both gradual development and saltation. In the example of the anorexic woman, the gradual evolution to a new order was the rule, although from time to time there were also leaps. For example, one day, the woman in question suddenly found that she liked certain kinds of food better than others and that she had been eating things she did not really like for years. The insight was a flash: she acted upon it, readjusting her eating according to the preferences she had so suddenly discovered. As a result, she found that she vomited much less often.

In some cases, the saltation principle is even more impressive. We can be proceeding with patience, allowing for time to do its work when, unexpectedly, after a long phase of what seemed to be dormancy, a jump takes place. I am thinking here of a young man whose contact problems had prevented him from finding a group of people with whom he could spend his free time. He sat at home watching television and had been doing so for the past ten years since he had left home and got an apartment of his own. We spoke of the problem, trying to discover its sources and mechanisms, the conflicts out of which it grew. One day he met a woman in a café and suddenly the man discovered his sociability. He became open, made contacts; he felt more at ease while talking to people; now and again he even initiated conversations. It was not as if he had not met other women before, but obviously the time was ripe: the hundred years of sleep were over; the charm was broken and the young man awakened to take part in life.

The butterfly principle

The butterfly principle in human beings is most readily observable on the level of society. Here we have been unfortunate enough to experience the enormous and unpredictable effects of seemingly minor causes on a world-wide scale. One need only think here of the First World War, which was triggered by a relatively insignificant event. But, as the principle states, the situation was basically so unstable as to be threatened by a butterfly flapping its wings. The assassination at Sarajevo of the Austro–Hungarian prince, Franz Ferdinand, on 28 June 1914 led to unpredictable results of major consequence.

On the level of individuals we can distinguish three different applications of this principle. Generalized instability can lead to the eruption of the butterfly principle in (1) transition phases; (2) exceptional psychic and physical states; and (3) when unconscious complexes are touched. The first case we have already discussed as the biological phases of transition. During these moments of heightened instability, seemingly minor events can lead an individual into unpredictable chaos. All too often disputes in adolescence provoke major crises: suicides at this age have marked our period in history as well as earlier ones. Recently we have become particularly aware of the 'mid-life crisis'. This was an added factor of instability in the case of the 40-year-old businessman we spoke of above. Old age and retirement are similarly unstable moments: a minor change in an elderly person's life, like the closing down of his or her favourite café, can provoke a major crisis. Accustomed over years to meeting friends there, this closure can endanger the individual's lifestyle and threaten to destroy the order which he or she holds dear. As in the case of the old man who lost his job, finding new order at such times is very difficult.

We are also faced with instability in exceptional states. In panic, under shock, one can react in a completely unpredictable and exaggerated manner. Also, unaccustomed anger or extraordinary pressure can provoke extreme reactions which we do not recognize in ourselves. At the slightest prompting, one 'flies off the handle', doing or saying things that are quite atypical and unexpected. Exceptional states can also be triggered by a lack of sleep, of food, or a prolonged period of exhaustion, either physical or mental. One often notices how, just before vacation, or perhaps at the beginning of a three-week holiday, couples have heated disagreements about insignificant details which, at the time, seem very important. When we are fatigued the butterfly principle often applies: we tend to be overly sensitive, irritable, unstable: a glance, a word, a gesture is enough to start off a huge row.

We also observe the butterfly principle at work when unconscious complexes are touched. The level of consciousness is then lowered: one's psychic energy is drained off into the unconscious and one becomes destabilized. Extreme and unpredictable reactions can then be triggered. For example, Charlie, who will be described in Chapter 5, had a serious authority complex, i.e. a problem with authority. He was unconcious of it. Whenever he encountered an authority figure, he flared up and acted in unpredictable ways. As he gained more knowledge of this complex through therapy, Charlie became progressively less prone to grave destabilizations in situations which had previously been 'dangerous' for him. The more unconscious the complex, the more one is ruled by the butterfly principle when the complex is touched.

Also, the more unconscious complexes one possesses, the more *generally* unstable one tends to be. Sabena, who will also be described in Chapter 5, was one such person. She lived very much in the dark about her inner world and had not come to differentiate the various elements of her unconscious life. She was not aware of her complexes, and her conscious perception of what went on in and around her was severely restricted: she was, therefore, often destabilized in many different life situations.

The example of narcissistic personalities offers impressive proof of the importance of the butterfly principle and its relation to the level of consciousness. These people who have a poorly developed sense of self-esteem are, as Kathrin Asper (1987) has noted, generally unaware of the deep wounding to which they were subjected in their early childhood. They have no memories of what happened to them and led to the birth of their complex of negative self-esteem. They are unconscious of the complex itself and become quickly destabilized whenever it is touched. That is, they are extraordinarily sensitive to criticism. Life with them can be very difficult, for their extreme reactions to minor events seem inexplicable.

I am thinking in this context of a teacher, a very good teacher, devoted to her work and to her students. She never married and teaching was the main content of her life. She was loved and admired, but also feared by her students and colleagues. For she was not only very gifted, she was also unusually sensitive to criticism. Whenever she got the impression that her work was not being duly appreciated, she flew into uncontrolled rage and was subsequently filled with bitterness.

This example is quite typical: such people are often extraordinarily gifted and tend to give their best. They need to, for their sense of self-worth depends on being appreciated for their efforts. At the same time, they repeatedly react in extreme and unexpected ways when they sense a wound to their self-esteem. This teacher, consequently, never married. Many people with such a disorder marry and remarry rather frequently. And their lives are marked by very dramatic events. If they do manage to live relatively 'normal' lives for long stretches at a time, it is often at the cost of their milieu. Family and friends are repeatedly subjected to their virulent and incomprehensible attacks of rage whenever the person feels slighted. Such situations are particularly hurtful for their children who, as a result of this completely unpredictable parent with his or her rages and sulks, grow up with deep insecurities.

Other more spectacular cases of the butterfly principle in narcissistic personalities are reported in the daily press. Suddenly a man, a well-respected citizen, for example, faced with his wife's infidelity or 'unjustly' dismissed from his work, murders those whom he considers responsible for this deep insult to his self-esteem. Such a man may have managed to live a 'normal' life until this point. But the event which sparks him off so riles him, touching his deeply wounded and insecure sense of self-esteem, that he suddenly behaves in a completely exaggerated and unpredictable manner.

Actually, this aspect of the butterfly principle is very often at work, but in some lucky cases the individuals manage to realize the disproportionality of their fantasized reaction. They can allow the fantasy to be without having to act on it. A man, aged 30, was plagued with such a sensitivity on one point especially. He felt unable to defend himself. And so, whenever he had the feeling that he was being treated in a disdainful manner, he withdrew into a dynamite-laden silence. He was extremely timid and would never have dared to live out the scenes which he then saw before his inner eye. For he fantasized dramatic ways of torturing and triumphing over whomever had so riled him. His fantasies were so sadistic that he was even ashamed of telling them. In therapy we were able to talk of them, examining their content and discovering their essential compensatory qualities. As long as the man really could not defend himself in an adequate way, and remained closed off in his wounded silence, his fantasies were necessary. Gradually, however, through this process of recognition, he dared to make more realistic and appropriate attempts at self-defence: his fantasies began to take up less and less room in his life. With time they just disappeared. I must, however, add here, that other cases exist in which people whose lives are dominated by the butterfly principle do not act out their fantasies, but are none the less unable to confront and integrate the psychic material they contain.

Instability

As we saw in the last section, the degree of instability to which we are subject depends on how conscious we are of ourselves and our conflicts or complexes. The more we know about them and their dynamics, the less extremely destabilized we tend to become. Relative stability requires relative awareness. Small children and infants, incapable of conscious reflection, are, accordingly, basically unstable. They are also, therefore, eminently adaptable. But their adaptation takes place in an automatic manner, perhaps even according to something like cellular necessity (like the thermodynamic systems in far from equilibrium states).

The stability of adults depends on their level of consciousness. In the cases examined above (in which instability arose when a critical point was reached) the people in question were all more or less unconscious of the conflicts underlying their behaviour patterns. We can think back to the woman who was entirely unaware of the difficulties separations caused her. Therefore, whenever an outward occurrence triggered her hidden fear, she was seriously destabilized. The unconscious conflicts of adulthood can all be traced back to early childhood adaptive patterns. At the time the child adopted the pattern it was necessary and appropriate. But our life circumstances change and we outgrow our old patterns of behaviour. If, however, we do not manage to let go of antiquated ways of acting and reacting in time, they get in the way of our development: we persist in an old order and cannot find a new one that suits our present lives and needs. The woman we are speaking of here was living with such an old, outdated adaptive pattern. It had developed very early on because of basic instabilities she felt in her parents' marriage. The parents had an unsatisfying relationship and the child sensed this, although no strong words were spoken. As a result she developed fears of separation which served to reassure her of her parents' presence. She used to be so frightened of going away, of a parent leaving, of being sent away, that her concerned parents began to pay special attention to her. They reassured her, comforted her, and tended to leave her alone less often. And they stayed together, perhaps partially because of their child's fears of being abandoned.

This pattern in no way corresponded to the woman's adult life. Her marriage was relatively secure and there was no real, imminent danger of abandonment. But her unconscious (and, therefore, unresolved) 'separation complex', as we can call it, made her become exceedingly anxious and dependent. She could not grow up to be a relatively autonomous adult while living with those childhood fears which she automatically transposed onto her present life. As noted when commenting on her 'chaos scenario', in psychotherapy we were concerned with raising this material (and its long buried roots in childhood) to consciousness. The woman became increasingly aware of her complex and of the various ways in which she had automatically learned to deal with it as a child. As a result, she came to acquire a certain degree of autonomy and her fears of separation diminished. She had become 'sensitized' to her problem and accordingly, was less extremely destabilized when it was touched in the course of her daily life.

Sensitivity and flexibility

As we have seen in the last section, adaptations in maturity depend on our ability to notice and reflect on ourselves and the situations we are faced with. We can then make conscious decisions about how we feel we can and want to adapt. Basic to such mature adaptive processes is our sensitivity to what is going on inside ourselves and in our environment. We have to be able to sense alterations in our inner and outer worlds, becoming aware of change and instabilities as they arise. Then and only then can we realize our needs and try to deal with them in an adequate and satisfying manner.

In psychotherapy we try to develop sensitivity and awareness as tools for adaptation. This is not a simple matter. For often, in the course of development, a withdrawal has taken place. As we saw in the preceding example, once an adaptation has been found, the individual can continue with it, oblivious to the changes that have taken place. People see before them images of the past and not those of the present. It is as if they were no longer able to perceive what they really have before them. Their sensitive pores of perception have been closed off. Unclogging them means getting involved in life again and allowing themselves to be touched by what is seen and experienced.

A woman with whom I had just recently begun working reported how raw and sensitized she felt since beginning therapy. She felt more than she used to feel: she was more easily moved and touched by what she saw and heard around her. Such developments are typical, if the work goes well. They are probably partially responsible for what people who have undergone therapy describe as 'being able to enjoy life more'.

As will become clear in our next and final chapter, the development of sensitivity as a tool for adaptation entails raising to consciousness various things that go on within oneself and in the outside world. We shall examine there the case of Mrs X, who became increasingly sensitive to the first signs of her migraine headaches coming on. Through this sensitivity she managed to realize what was actually bothering her and causing her symptom. She could discover the conflicts to which she was reacting and could try to deal with them in a more effective way. She no longer had to get her headaches automatically (so that she could retreat). Instead she could face the conflicts and decide on how she *wanted* to react.

As we see here, flexibility is a direct result of increased sensitivity. One becomes able to find new adaptive patterns; noticing one's needs, one can reflect on and choose appropriate ways of dealing with them. This particular woman became an avid hiker and nature lover. She also opened up towards her family and discussed with them matters which gave rise to inner conflict and which she had previously kept to herself and suffered with in silence (but not without a great deal of bitterness and resentment). Flexibility means the broadening of one's spectrum for acting and reacting.

The necessity of sensitivity and flexibility for adaptation is as clear in psychology as it is in natural science. Nevertheless, their attainment is sometimes not feasible. People can persist in an old and unadapted order and remain inflexible and insensitive (or unable to put their sensitivity to good use). In nature, such systems either remain in a death-like stasis until more favourable conditions arise or they merely die out. Every day some species on earth is erased forever. As for individual human beings, we seem to have more choices. Some people, like Edith, actually do die, unable to free themselves from their unliveable order. Others withdraw from life into illness – think of the young schizophrenic boy, and Odintsov's depressions. And still others retreat emotionally for the rest of their lives: this was Odintsov's later fate.

But we have one more choice. People living in society can resist their own adaptation, but in this way force their milieu to adapt. Not infrequently we find families in which one member is particularly inflexible. Invariably then, the problem of finding a new order is transferred to another member of the family. It is often a child who, in becoming physically or mentally ill, becomes both the symptom carrier and the prodding for the much needed but otherwise unobtainable change. Mrs X, of whom we have been speaking here, was such a case. Her own, personal order had become so inflexible and she was in such a state of stasis, that it took her daughter's illness to relieve the blockage. Only when her little girl got sick could Mrs X begin to conceive of the necessity of finding another kind of order.

Our excursion into the field of chaos and order as science perceives them today has serious implications for us. If out of the experience of chaos, order can emerge, and if this can only come about through our sensitivity to the need for change, then sensitivity acquires a major importance in human life. This is quite contrary to popular ideal images of humanity. Furthermore, if the communication of the various parts of our system – our bodies and minds, as well as our network of social relationships – is actually a complex interaction of elements pressing for new adaptations, then these messages – I am thinking here especially of the physical symptoms – are of fundamental value for us. Such a point of view is quite contrary to contemporary efforts to control and silence this communication, for example with medication. The image of balance and calm which dominates our stereotype of a well-adjusted individual today is quite the opposite of what we have learned here. Rather, a finely developed capacity to sense instabilities (imbalance and disturbance) and to reflect on them best serves the vital needs of individual human beings capable of adequate adaptations to the demands of their particular life.

The people who can let order emerge from chaos would be particularly open to being touched by the world within and without and capable of examining their situation, judging their own ability and willingness to adapt – with the help of their conscious mind. As we shall see in Chapter 5, the confrontation with chaos is a uniquely communicative process. Science also underlines the importance of communication as a means of transformation. Here is the exact point at which our examples in Chapter 3 failed. They withdrew from contact both with the outer world and with the divergent aspects of their inner world.

One of the reasons why psychotherapy works may well be the fact that it re-establishes communicative activity. One begins to talk and thus to reflect again on oneself, with the therapist and ultimately, with one's milieu. One also enters into the communicative processes going on inside oneself. One contacts and begins to listen to the various aspects of one's being. Not unimportant in this dialogue is the contact with the reality principle. When the work begins, this principle may lie mainly in the therapist. With his or her distance, he or she has the necessary perspective to view the situation in a more realistic way. He or she can confront and question, for example, the overblown fantasies and the restrictive order to which the individual has become so accustomed that they are 'a matter of fact' for him. As the work proceeds, the reality function is increasingly internalized: the individual becomes capable of continuing the dialogue with it on their own.

In Chapter 5 the ways in which psychotherapy encounters chaos and goes on from there to seek the kind of natural, organic order that scientists observe in nature will be described in detail. Unlike the rigid and restrictive order which excludes chaos, this order is flexible. And instead of blocking the development of life, it supports it.

Chapter 5

The psychotherapeutic chaos encounter and the search for organic order

This final chapter is devoted to the practical application of what we have discovered in the preceding pages. We shall elucidate here the psychotherapeutic approach to chaos, based on the conviction that, met in the appropriate way, chaos can prove to be fruitful. The critical moment of its eruption can mark a beginning: the beginning of a search for another kind of order. This order is more suited to the individual and his needs and shows a high degree of chaos tolerance. It corresponds to the image of order that scientists observe in nature.

The first part of the chapter deals with translating the concept of 'organic order' (Weiss 1973) to the realm of human experience. We can think of it in terms of retrieving the natural flexibility of the point of view. The withdrawal and distance which goes hand in hand with adherence to a rigid order and a narrow self-image can be complemented by the proximity of direct experience. This closer perspective favours the development of sensitivity: one becomes aware of diverse feelings, states of being. It is as if they were all expressing points of view which we can proceed to consider and distinguish, judging their relevance within our wider personality. Thus, the self-image becomes more complex, multi-faceted and broader. The resultant order corresponds to the individual and his or her specific needs; it permits the person to attain flexibility in the face of changing life circumstances.

In the second part of the chapter we shall take a close look at the practice of psychotherapy, pointing out the ways in which we attempt to deal with the initial chaos experience and go on from there to stimulate the development of organic order. We accept and examine the chaotic situation and work at discerning its underlying patterns. We try to encourage the development of sensitivity to the inner world by paying close attention to feelings, images, dreams, and the body. The direct, experiential contact and subsequent examination of this material helps us to encounter and comprehend chaos and, at the same time, encourages the expansion of the personality into its own own, unique order.

In a third and final section, two types of cases which differ from those discussed above will be examined. In the one, the ultimate goal of the work cannot be the search for organic order. In the other, the presenting problem is not chaos. Some people, faced with chaos, are not ready or able to pursue the psychological work of finding an order of their own. Their need is, rather, to retrieve the sense of security offered by their habitual – through restrictive – order. Sometimes, at a later date, they can and do take up the search for organic order, but often their single chaos experience remains a traumatic event which they do their best to try and forget. In practice we also occasionally meet other people who do not come into psychotherapy because of a chaotic experience. Sent by family or friends, they have no specific complaints. Early on in the treatment we discover that they too distance themselves from chaos, but with more success than the majority of cases. Often harbouring deep fears of order, they tend to focus on the inimical forces of order they see all around them, and thus, avoid contact with their own inner chaos. But they also deny their own, archetypal human need for order. Work with such people follows the same pattern as in the earlier examples. The body plays an especially important role here: it serves to anchor their uncertain perceptions of themselves in their physical being, and thus to confirm the reality of these perceptions.

ORGANIC ORDER IN MAN

In the preceding chapter we discovered a model of order existing in nature that is extremely different from that which we observed in individual people faced with chaos. This order reveals an extra-ordinary chaos tolerance, for chaos can be a stage in the evolution from one form of order to the next. In this connection we saw how systems – including the human body – could adapt to altered conditions by going through a chaotic phase in which their component elements were said to communicate.

The biologist Paul Weiss (1973) goes so far as to say that nature's order is 'kaleidoscopic'. Natural organisms are in a continual state of flux and flow. Open to influences from without and within, they sense alterations in conditions and adapt to them, seeking the optimal order for the new circumstances. The capacity for adaptation to ever-changing conditions depends on the system's sensitivity and flexibility.

As part of nature, we, too, basically possess organic order that enables us to adapt physiologically and psychologically to the modifications in our life circumstances. As we mentioned in Chapter 4, this order might well be *grounded* in our physical bodies: that would help explain the frequent physical symptoms which arise when a need for change becomes urgent. But the necessary prerequisite for flexible adaptation is our awareness of, our sensitivity to, the needs which make themselves felt. This preliminary openness however, is, often lacking. Again and again in the preceding pages we have come to see how people tend to retreat from chaotic experience into a world of rigid order which inevitably corresponds to a narrow self-image: various emotions and aspects of the personality cannot be accepted as part of a larger whole. Thus jealousy and envy, disappointment and fear, failure and separation are excluded from the way individuals see themselves and the world. But, rejecting these facts of life, these undeniable realities of human existence, leads to a severe restriction: as a result, the breadth and flexiblity of the personality suffers. In addition, the emotional withdrawal which accompanies such restrictive order makes individuals incapable of sensing what is going on in and outside themselves. Unable to sense their needs, they cannot find satisfying fulfilment of them.

In psychotherapy we are concerned with stimulating sensitivity as a vitally important tool, and thus, with retrieving the natural flexibility of the personality. As Jung so well said, his therapeutic goal was to find 'a state of fluidity, change and growth where nothing is eternally fixed and hopelessly petrified' (1953–79, XVI: 99). At the end of the process, the person discovers that he or she is 'someone far more rounded and complete'. But this means 'assimilating all sorts of things into the sphere of [the] personality' which the person previously rejected 'as disagreeable or even impossible' (1953–79, XII: 84).

In Jung's terms, the integrative process of therapy is stimulated by the self. It is the psychic instance which favours and promotes the ability to become aware of – and, therefore, eventually, to integrate – divergent elements of the personality. When we become too narrow-minded and one-sided (as we generally tend to do) the self draws our attention to other aspects of ourselves which we have come to neglect. It does so by producing symptoms (physical and psychic, illnesses, dreams, even accidents). They demand attention, forcing our conscious mind to examine them. We thus come to realize previously unknown (i.e. unconscious) material. We can then consider and differentiate it, judging its importance within the wider context of our being. In this way our restricted and restrictive comprehension of ourselves is broadened.

Mario Jacoby (1980: 219–20) expressed this integrative work in terms which are helpful for us here. He took the symbol of the circle to describe the way in which we try to examine conflictual material. We reflect and meditate on it, circling it: from each new standpoint things look different. And so, we come to see a problem not from one, but from various points of view. Such a process helps to relativize the conscious, ego point of view and gives us a sense of greater flexibility and freedom.

The search for organic order in human beings can be described as a continual and never-ending process of trying to become aware of the diverse points of view which dwell within us. We can, of course, never exhaust the pool of our unconscious points of view, but we can try to be as open for them as is possible at each given moment. This attention to one's own variant ways of seeing and feeling necessarily leads to an expansion (and, also a strengthening) of the personality. The new order is less exclusive than the old: the foundations on which we stand are, consequently, broader and more stable. Increased flexibility and adaptability are gained through the process.

The portrait of a woman by Picasso (Figure 5.1) corresponds well to the type of multi-faceted image which results. On the one hand, we do recognize a woman; on the other, the portrait is odd, with its combination of different planes in one figure. The difficulty we have in accepting such an image of a woman, or of ourselves, is reflected in the shock which Picasso's first cubist painting created on the public: the *Demoiselles d'Avignon* created a major scandal when it was exhibited for the first time in 1906. James Joyce's *Ulysses* (1912) made a similarly bad impression on the general public. Its unconventional narrative technique interweaves different points of view – of different characters, as well as of inner and outer worlds – without any concern for relating a logically coherent story.

The unusual type of coherency which reigns both in cubism and in multiple point of view narration (like Joyce's *Ulysses*, Faulkner's *The Sound and the Fury*, or in certain films: *Rashomon*, *L'Année Dernière à Marienbad*) is potentially confusing: their conglomeration of perspectives forms an image which is bizarre and unsettling.

Likewise, our own multiple points of view, combining different and not always reconcilable images into a broader whole, do not correspond to the simpler images we cherish of ourselves.

Figure 5.1 Pablo Picasso, Seated Woman (1941), National Gallery of Modern Art, Munich

Consequently, we do not find it easy to integrate them. Actually we seem to tend to form self-images of conventional coherency which are relatively narrow and uni-dimensional.

As we noted in Chapter 4, the narrowing of the self-image generally stems from early childhood adaptations when the extraordinarily malleable (and unstable) child finds a way of being that helps him or her to survive. We can say that the child learns to identify with certain points of view, to conform to them, and to their concommitant expectations. The process begins very early on in life. It can be called a 'process of selective perception'. Initially, infants see only a chaotic and undistinguished mass. With time their biological development enables them to focus, to pick out individual objects within their field of vision. The first images they perceive are merely sketchy outlines, the hair line and the position of the eyes of faces close-by. But as they grow, their capacity for perceiving detail grows too. They can focus on and distinguish people and objects. One would then expect that increasing mobility and the joy in movement and play would lead the child to explore new and ever-changing points of view. This is most likely what happens – in part. But there is also a distinct and parallel tendency towards the restriction of the point of view. For a long time children focus on their parents' way of seeing the world, imitating and emulating these models. They orient themselves according to them, and thus, gain a sense of security. When they go off to school, other models and points of view are added to their spectrum: those of the teacher, of the 'do's and don'ts' of the school and the social system, for they are young and learning members, being initiated into the world of society. And so, children learn to focus their attention on what the teacher is saying up at the front instead of on whatever they might accidentally also be hearing from other parts of the room. The buzzing of a bee at the classroom window, a melody filtering in from the class next door, must all take second place to what the school authorities consider important. At home, too, they learn to distinguish right from wrong, good from bad. Often they adopt their parents' points of view. The peer group offers the possibility of learning other values, but for a long time they are a reflection of what the children have learned in their respective homes. We are, in our development from early childhood on, naturally engaged in a learning process: that of coming to perceive and evaluate in a selective manner, according to the value systems agreed upon by our milieu. Although a certain amount of individuality gets lost in the process, the development of the ego and a sense of security and identity seem to require such an experience.

Via identification with the collective points of view, we learn to adapt to life, but simultaneously to control, sometimes to ignore other impulses, fantasies, desires, feelings, ideas, and even personality traits which are 'unacceptable'. As they are disapproved of by our milieu, we come to reject them as useless, unimportant, impractical, unreasonable, or just plain 'not right'.

The emotional rewards for comformity are great, but they can often be too binding. The approval, love, security, and the sense of continuity and identity that such identification guarantees are counteracted when new life situations require more flexibility. This was the case, for example, for the businessman who had been treating himself for years in the same way as his father had treated him: he demanded and expected a great deal of himself. But he pushed so hard that he actually could no longer go on: he had a nervous collapse. Although the relationship with his real father had never really been good, the identification with him and with his points of view gave the young boy a sense of security and identity. It is often far more important for a child to survive emotionally within the family than to assert his or her individuality. And so, it may be only when chaos erupts that we are forced to realize that we have come to a dead-end. Our old, adopted points of view prove insufficient for our present life circumstances. We need to recover the natural flexibility of our personality.

In this regard we can call chaos the moment when the various and divergent points of view which have been long repressed or have never become conscious make themselves felt and heard. They find expression in fantasies, thoughts, feelings, moods, memories, associations, dreams, as well as in physical sensations, pains, and illnesses. In terms of our scientific model, these are our component parts which, sensing that a critical point has been reached, begin to communicate. They are aiming at finding a new and more suitable order that corresponds to modified, present needs. If we can enter into the communicative processes, transformation becomes possible. We realize other points of view, can reflect on them, and take them into consideration in our efforts to discover appropriate and satisfying ways of acting and reacting in the here and now. In this way, our order becomes dynamic, helping us to adjust to new life situations as they arise. It can then be called kaleidoscopic and organic, for it is 'chaos inclusive': it takes the chaotic into account, considering its potentially valuable points of view instead of spontaneously rejecting them.

PSYCHOTHERAPY

In psychotherapy we work, on the one hand, at getting directly involved in the communicative processes at hand, zooming in on experience and allowing it to move us. On the other hand, we seek distance, for, as our scientific model stressed, we need to find the proper perspective to be able to discern order in chaos.

The distanced perspective helps to disperse darkness and order chaos. Our critical distance enables us to examine events and see their logical and psycho-logical connections. We can understand what happened, naming and analysing the mechanisms. We discover repetitive ways of acting and reacting that belong to us, behaviour patterns. Thus we gain insights into our deeper motivations. Verbalizing our confused feelings and impressions also helps us to gain distance from chaos. In putting our despair into words, we render it communicable and reduce its intolerable dimensions, its overpowering quality. Chaos that can be ex-pressed, described, is robbed of its unspeakable, forbidden, and foreboding aspect. The temporal perspective likewise serves to reduce chaos's terrors. We can line up events and perceive their development. We can also recall other difficult moments and the ways in which we managed to handle them. Thinking of the ineluctable passage of time, we can realize that our suffering necessarily has temporal limitations: it is not everlasting and will one day be a thing of the past. Our human gifts of speech and rational thinking permit us to find distance from chaos: we can face it and examine it, learning to conquer the monsters of the deep. But as we have noted, especially in conclusion to Chapter 3, when distance is not complemented by close, direct experience, it is merely defensive withdrawal. It leads to retreat from the world at large into autistic order and to a total divorce from one's own emotional reality. It ends in rationalization which is identical to petrification.

One major difficulty in working with chaos is the panic it can cause. At times it is so extreme that the main, underlying problems must take second place for some time. Fear then so dominates the person that lowering its level to a tolerable degree becomes the prime concern in the initial phase. In some cases, medication must be precribed; in others it is, however, possible to gain the necessary distance from chaos and the fear it provokes without having to resort to drugs. Finding this distance depends on achieving the right mixture of proximity to the individual and distance from chaos.

Clients must sense that their therapist accepts them, together with their fears and insecurities. Feeling thus accepted in a moment in which one rejects oneself or feels rejected is an important 'holding' experience. It is comparable to a child's being held in its mother's arms. His or her problems do not then just disappear, but the child is soothed and comforted when he or she can get from the mother the impression that it is 'all right' anyway. Chaos is definitely less threatening when one feels held in this way. Such a maternally caring attitude is the model for the intra–psychic acceptance of chaos which therapy strives to stimulate.

At the same time, we strive for distance through realization. As we mentioned above, clients need to acquire the assurance that their chaotic moments will not overwhelm them. The threat must be reduced, so that they can come to feel that there are problems here, but that they can be dealt with. Chaos becomes containable. The reassurance that order can emerge from it, that it can prove to be a meaningful event in one's life, is all important. Individuals who turn to psychotherapy already have a certain degree of this confidence, otherwise they would not have bothered to consult a therapist. As the work progresses, new chaotic experiences can and do arise. But their repeated encounter leads, in time, to an increased confidence in one's ability to handle them. The fears which used to appear as from nowhere can be faced. They are no longer unpredictable bandits who turn up from nowhere and render us helpless. But this type of approach takes time, for the conflicts underlying our fears are all relatively unconscious. They are deeply buried in the past: retrieving them from the dark domains of the unknown requires very concentrated efforts.

In modern management terminology one can say that therapy is the training ground for chaos encounter. Within this privileged space, time is set aside for the 'dilation of the moment'. The divergent, seemingly useless perceptions which flow together in our experience of reality are allowed to surface and to add their information to the personality. In the empty spaces of therapy – its silences, its non–directedness – this 'unproductive' material (be it memories, sensations, fantasies, moods, feelings, associations, images, or even ideas) is granted attention. It becomes the stuff of which the personality is made, parts of a puzzle which go on to seek their special coherency in the organic order of a unique, complex, and multi-faceted individual.

But how do we move from the initial chaos experience which brings someone to therapy to the final expansion of the personality in a new order with increased chaos tolerance? The path leads from the discovery of the old, habitual order and what so disturbed its harmony through the realms of the emotions, images, and the imagination, and their physical correspondences.

The image and the imagination

The image and the imagination are especially helpful in stimulating contact with lost layers of the personality. This domain, which Paul Claudel (in a 1984 radio interview) associated with disorder (in contrast to thinking-order), evokes the less linear, less rational, and therefore, opens up communication with this other side of our being.

The image moves with a force and power rarely found in the word. Ancient cultures were well aware of this fact, as Judaism's prohibition of making images of God well shows. Catholicism's vibrant imagery had the power to touch and move masses of people. This provoked Protestantism's '*Bilder Sturm*' – a violent battle against the communication through imagery. Our age continues to testify to the power of the image: television and its cult of the image captured the fantasy of millions, from the poorest slums to the most opulent palaces the world over, and that within the space of twenty-five years.

Via the image and the making of images – the imagination – we bring the abstract, the intangible, within our own reach. In a way, we gain power over it. Both the making of images of divinities (idols) and the voodoo doll can be said to serve this purpose. But, for modern 'civilized' men and women, too, the image remains a medium which captivates.

Jung (1953–79, VI: 754) spoke of the 'generative power' of the image. As we shall see in our example, the image can stimulate contact with one's inner self. In therapy, therefore, we often work with it, encouraging the attention to images in fantasies, both waking and dreaming. The direct emotional contact with the material is what counts.

Anne had reached the ultimate in chaos intolerance and unbending order several times before I met her. She was 21 and had already tried to take her life several times. Sent by her mother, she did not seem very eager to get involved in therapy. She would enter, walking in a stiff, almost zombie-like fashion, sit down and withdraw into silence. When I tried to encourage her to speak, she would answer in a flat tone of voice and in monosyllables. Her facial expression remained unchanging. Then she would return to her stone-faced silence. It took several months before Anne decided to tell me about her attempted suicides and what had prompted them. On all three occasions she had felt – as she still did today – that there was no sense in going on: the problems she was facing seemed irresolvable. She had not completed any formal education nor been trained for any profession because she had often been ill between the ages of 12 and 18. She had consequently missed so much school that she was always too far behind to catch up. Also, having been out of school so much, she had no real close relationships with her peers: she had no friends, and what bothered her the most, no boy friends. She was living at home and saw no chance of leaving; she could not possibly get a job and support herself.

Anne was at a dead-end: she saw no way out. And, as long as one remained within her frame of thinking, there really was no escape. The logical consequence was the impossibility of change and thus the impossibility of going on. This is 'dead-end logic' which often dominates depressive states. Everything seems black and hopeless. Once one accepts the basic premise, that no order can arise from chaos, then all falls logically into place. Anne had withdrawn into a static and sterile world in which communication had ceased to take place. Its rigid and narrow order was determined by logic and causality. As she had taken her distance from the world at large, no actual life experiences could help Anne nuance her black-and-white image. Her order remained harmonious, for it closed off the perception of anything that did not fit. In a way, she had become insensitive: she could not sense other things going on in her inner or outer world. Her thinking, but also her emotional and physical expression had become rigid and inflexible.

Anne's incommunicative manner in the therapeutic situation well reflected the lack of communication within. But how to stimulate communication, movement, involvement, the flow of life again? Trying to engage her in conversation did not work. But one day, Anne seemed to become reanimated. She entered the hour as usual, showing no special signs of agitation or excitement, but reported that a young man had followed her to my office. She made no comment on the event, reporting it in her withdrawn and detached fashion. It seemed to me that such an occurrence was likely to move her, but when I asked Anne how she felt about what had happened, she just said, plainly and flatly, and without varying the tone of her voice in any way, 'unpleasant'. I then asked her what the scene would have looked like had she and the young man been animals. Anne seemed to awake as from a deep sleep. Slowly she began to describe a lively, multicoloured scene. The description did not come bubbling out of her, it took time for her to get involved in it, but she gradually did so. She saw herself as a princess and the young man as a fox. And, as I asked more and more about the imaginary scene, she went on, describing in ever greater detail the fairy tale she saw before her inner eye. The scene became more and more nuanced. From a simple 'unpleasant' event we arrived at a pluri-valent being followed, being of interest, being capable of love and transformation. The flat black-and-white newspaper style of the initial report became a colourful and imaginative experience in which Anne could make out and describe a wide range of feelings.

What happened here? Anne's imagination was touched by the image. She became lively and communicative; the irrational entered: other aspects of her being came to the fore. Within the image she discovered herself as a being with complex and divergent emotional states and needs. She could imagine transformation. Her stone-faced nonchalance gave way to a deep sensitivity. Indulging in her imagination, bathing in the image, Anne felt able to open up, to allow communication to take place with herself and with me. Her inflexible imprisonment in a drab and dead-end life could be given up, for the space of the hour at least, in favour of a living fantasy of other possibilities.

This experience marked the beginning of Anne's retrieving her natural flexibility and re-establishing contact with her inner and outer world. A process of sensitization had begun. After this session, Anne continued to arrive in her closed manner, but with little encouragement, she would describe in images whatever was preoccupying her. Sometimes she chose to draw or paint pictures at home and to bring them to the hours, but mostly she just came and told of her experiences as if they were pictures she saw before her inner eye.

After two years, Anne had acquired such a sensitivity to herself and her needs through the pictures she described in therapy, that she began to perceive other possibilities. She had heard from a friend of her mother's that a job as a salesgirl was available in a boutique for young people and wanted to see what it was like. Evidently her fantasy was touched by this idea, for, as she wrote to me some time afterwards, she became interested in fashion design, began to draw models of clothing, and set up a little designer-seamstress shop.

The image continued to play an important role in her life. And when we think back to the desperation which was so clearly written on her immobile face at the beginning of our work, it was the capacity for forming images, for getting involved in them and letting herself be moved by them, that had been so terribly missing in her life before. Being able to imagine other possibilities was the key which opened the door of communication between this young woman and her own inner self and the world around her. The process took time; it revealed the non-linearity (the complexity) of Anne's being and it helped her to become aware of her critical points, the situations which made her feel unstable, insecure. From this woman's chaos experiences, the path went through a rigid and inflexible order, into a communicative phase, until the new order – of a life with images and independence emerged.

In the work with Anne the distanced perspective, in the sense of attempting to perceive the patterns underlying her chaos, was of minor importance. It seemed that she had become so distanced from the world of direct experience that encouraging contact with it was of the utmost urgency. Nor did Anne feel the need to understand the processes which she was going through. She apparently needed to reimmerse herself in life and rediscover its colours and perfumes – or even discover them for the first time – for the cloud of doom had been hanging over her for as long as she could remember. Immersion in the flow of her imagination (the realm of chaos, according to Claudel) awakened this young woman to the movement and the e-motion of life.

The dream

Like the imaginative fantasies of waking hours, those of the night provide the opportunity of contacting other aspects of the person-ality. In working with them, we are mainly interested in making the experience come alive, in seeking the direct contact with the material. This communicative process fosters the sensitization of individuals to their needs and to parts of themselves of which they are less conscious.

When working with dreams, we invariably witness a characteristic 'emergence of order out of chaos': People almost always introduce their dreams with words like, 'I had a funny dream' or a 'crazy dream', or some such phrase showing the extent to which they are confronted with meaningless confusion in what they experienced during the night. At times they are so upset by this bizarreness that they cannot get further involved in the dream, are not even able to try to describe, discern, or distinguish what happened in it. Sabena, who will be described in more detail at the end of this chapter, rejected her dreams in this way; she could seldom manage to go beyond her initial shock at such chaotic information. However, when one does apply conscious attention to the dream, associations, memories, and feelings arise which help us to realize that the dream not only 'makes sense', but also proffers new and unexpected points of view which can be of relevance for us.

Order emerges from chaos as we apply our conscious faculties to discerning the component elements of the dream (of chaos). But, of course, we must first become alert to their communication. Often we do not, simply forgetting what 'happened to us' in the night. Thus, in many therapies, dreams are never discussed.

In this section we shall examine three different types of dream and the role they played in making the dreamers realize aspects of themselves of which they were previously unaware. The categories correspond to Sonja Marjasch's (1961) differentiation between what she calls the 'dream ego' and the 'I in dreams'. Whereas, the latter shows the dreamers approximately as they are in reality, the former shows them quite different from their habitual way of being. The point of view expressed in the dream is then further from consciousness or represents a further stage in development. In the third type of dream, the 'I in dreams' becomes a 'dream ego', as another figure, or slightly altered conditions, make the dreamer capable (at the end of the dream) of doing 'the impossible', that is, of mastering a situation which is difficult for him or her in real life.

A banker, 35 years old, consulted me because he had had a frightening experience which did not fit in with the way he saw himself. He had felt nervous at a meeting and thought that he might faint. This idea was so unacceptable that he panicked. He did not faint, but became rather pale and weak. He made it through the meeting all right, managing quite well not to reveal his inner state. The next day he went to see his doctor who, after a thorough check up, suggested he come to see me.

Our work was devoted, in the preliminary phase, to finding out about the man's prevailing order and his chaos. The latter evidently had something to do with feeling nervous and weak: his ordering system could not encompass such feelings and needed to reject them. But the self-image which corresponds to such order is very limited. With no room allowed for weakness and nervousness, a personality is strikingly narrow and somehow unreal. Such traits belong to the range of what it means to be human and cannot be erased just because we wish to be otherwise. The fact that this order no longer suited the man and his needs is revealed by the symptoms which assailed him at this time. They became so loud and annoying as to get in the way of his functioning as he wished. But they also, and this is the positive aspect, so destabilized the man that he was prompted to reflect on himself. Thus, he reached a critical point which he apparently had never reached before. The man was under dire stress: his whole system – his psyche and also his body – began clamouring for a new and more liveable order.

Most helpful in enabling the man to examine his accustomed order and its actual unsuitability for him were his dreams. He dreamed regularly and reported his dreams in his twice-weekly sessions. On one occasion, after a particularly trying meeting during which he had done his best not to let any signs of weakness or nervousness surface, he had the following dream. He saw a group of people in theatrical costumes of former days. When he looked closer he realized that they were all made of straw and that he was one of them. This image is a very simple, even caricature-like representation, showing the 'I in the dream' as the man actually tried to appear in reality. He did his best to look 'correct', as if he were on stage and acting in accord with the expectations of the public. The inner emptiness that he was thus demanding of himself had never dawned on him before the dream. The fact that only straw figures, or puppets and dolls could look so impossibly perfect, whereas people naturally show signs of emotional states and imperfections, is well expressed in the image.

This dream was like a philosophical reflection on the man's ideal image of himself, as it showed him this ideal in such an extreme form that he was readily able to reflect on it. It offered a new angle, a new perspective on what had become an implicit and unexamined goal in life. Through his attention to the image, the man was able to take up the dialogue, to examine his habitual point of view and what it meant.

This type of dream is like a mirror of one's habitual way of being. It is, however, often such an exact representation of the way things are, of the way we behave, that we hardly take note of it. This dream has the advantage of being an exaggerated image. That makes it more fascinating, it draws our attention and holds it. It strikes and moves us.

Drawing the habitual, the implicit and accustomed (which is always more or less unconscious) into the light of consciousness and making it available for examination enables one to become aware of deeper dimensions of one's personality.

In the following dream this was achieved by reversal. The man was represented in the dream doing something he consciously definitely rejected, but which corresponded to long neglected needs. He dreamed that he was working in the bank late one night and took a large sum of money from the cash drawer. When he awoke he was absolutely shocked by his actions. They were terrible, impossible, shameful. How could he go on at the bank if he had such leanings? How could he be like that, even in a dream? These were some of the questions that plagued him. On discussing the dream in our next hour, the man expressed all of these qualms. But when I asked him how he had felt *in* the dream, we discovered equally intense emotions: he had felt exhilarated, joyful. The theft was an entirely pleasureable act. The extreme difference between these two emotional reactions – waking and sleeping – showed that we were in the presence of something new and important. The point of view depicted in the dream was very different from the man's conscious attitude. This aspect of his personality was very far from consciousness.

Here we see a 'dream ego', that is, according to Sonja Marjasch's (1961) categories, the dreamer appears substantially different from the way he or she usually sees him or herself. In considering the point of view of this 'dream ego', we came to discover many different layers of meaning. Its actions could be understood symbolically as representing the capacity for going out and getting, even taking, that which one needs. The man was not at all used to such direct, goal-oriented behaviour. He was not only conscientious in his work, he was also rather withdrawn and seldom made demands on his milieu. He did things for others but expressed no desire that they do the same for him. He seldom went out of his way to acquire or achieve something he might want, but waited in rather a passive fashion until the situation so presented itself that he could get what he wanted without appearing too 'eager' or 'demanding'. He had become passive, likeable, but lacked any aggressive behaviour. And, as the dream showed us – especially in the dream ego's joy at its act – at some level, a more aggressively-toned way of being did suit his needs. That is not to say that our banker, taking the dream's message to heart, quickly became an aggressive go-getter. He was too frightened of this kind of behaviour to make such a simple adjustment. Especially, he was afraid that if he did actually try to integrate this other, neglected aspect of himself that he would lose all love, respect, and support from his milieu. However, slowly but surely he began to make tentative approaches towards a more aggressive style. He first decided to take a course to learn to dance – something which he had long wanted to do, but had never dared. At the dance lessons he began to take the initiative more and more: this framework made it somehow easier for him to do so. After quite awhile, he also dared to show his teeth more in business situations. Through this dream and others he came to realize that his need to feel accepted had got in the way of his developing other, equally important sides of his personality.

In the following dream, which also shows a dream ego – quite different from the dreamer, at the end of the dream at least – we see how positive and supportive forces within our banker came to the fore. This type of dream is generally more easy to accept. For instead of showing the dreamer in a completely unusual – and perhaps unacceptable – way of being, it portrays him capable of something which he wishes were possible. One can speak here of wishful thinking, but examining the dream and taking the solution seriously, helps to reveal valuable ways of dealing with situations that are difficult in real life.

The man was at a meeting, 'shivering in his boots', as he put it. He felt very uncomfortable, under stress, anxious to perform well. Then an unknown man entered and approached him. He was tall and heavy, with a moustache. He radiated confidence and satisfaction, but in a very soothing way. The stranger looked him in the eye and touched him on the shoulder, then he went out of the room again. The dreamer sat there, a bit stunned, but full of good feelings about himself and his abilities. The subsequent meeting went very well, without any particular signs of nervousness or weakness. And the business was a success, too.

This dream shows us how also positive aspects of a personality can be be unconscious and undeveloped. The man had grown so accustomed to the fact that meetings were problematic for him that he was quite astounded that all could go so well, and that because of the appearance of the strange man. Reflecting on this helpful stranger, he came to associate him with an uncle he had not seen for many years. He looked like him, and he even radiated the same comforting feelings. He remembered then that this uncle had in fact tried to help him out, also acting in a supportive manner when he was in a stressful situation – at the end of high school and facing up-and-coming examinations. Throughout the years, he had no longer thought about his uncle. His sudden reappearance at this point in his life he took as a good sign. But he was mainly surprised, pleasantly so, at the dream and its outcome. He had managed, as if by magic, i.e with the help of this positive figure (and its new point of view), to master an otherwise difficult situation that he knew only too well. He was sceptical. He was pleased, but not convinced that such an evolution was possible. He had had too many negative experiences in real business meetings to be able to accept the dream as an eventual possibility.

Sometimes he did subsequently think of the dream, but he could not conceive of transposing it into real life until much later, when he felt stronger, and more encouraged by positive experiences. At that time, he tried to integrate this supportive element in reality. For him that meant that when he was in a meeting and feeling uncomfortable he would remind himself and evoke the image of his helpful uncle, even touching himself on the shoulder, and think of the comfort that he had drawn from that gesture in the dream. This imaginative approach gradually helped him to internalize the supportive figure. After five years of intensive therapy, the banker felt that he could go on on his own. He had his inner uncle; he had learned to become aware of his own needs for aggression and also other needs – for contact with other people and for a less stressful way of working. Whenever he noticed that he was feeling nervous or weak, he would examine the situation and try to understand what made him feel this way. He no longer spontaneously panicked, but accepted what was happening to him as reality. He was then able to confront the situation at hand, reassuring himself in an uncle-like way, and consider the real difficulties at hand. Sometimes he just went for a walk or relaxed in his office before a big meeting. He developed an order of his own, tuned into his own specific rhythms: it was flexible and based on a deepened sensitivity and awareness of himself and his needs, his feelings and the different points of view which made up his own, unique personality.

The body

Taking the body into consideration as a partner in communication with one's self is an essential and, at the same time, a difficult aspect of the therapeutic process. As we have seen above, our bodies often react when psychological change is needed. We sense something unusual: a disorder makes itself felt. Paying attention to these alterations helps us to tune into ourselves and our needs. Our bodies react to and reflect our psychological states (and vice versa): when we feel tense and under strain, our muscles become taut. When we are afraid we can find ourselves short of breath, our hearts beat faster, or we have digestive problems. We know that our bodies and our emotional states are related, but we frequently ignore and gloss over these interrelations. The therapeutic process aims at raising them to consciousness.

This means that we re-establish contact with the body as a valuable tool of self-awareness. We can think of it as an extremely sensitive seismograph, capable of registering the slightest instabilities. We learn to consult it and the sensations it picks up, for we want to try to comprehend the points of view that are thus being expressed. Coming to focus on this material, appreciating it as valid, even precious indications of our state of being, helps us to remain in touch with ourselves in an intimately nuanced manner. The process does a great deal to render physical 'symptoms' less frightening. The chaos caused by inexplicable tension and pain is, as with more obviously psychological symptoms, greatly lessened when these sensations are felt to be potentially meaningful. But not only negative, unpleasant body sensations tell us about ourselves. We can also feel relaxation, pleasure, enjoyment through increased awareness of muscle relaxation, calm breathing, feeling physically well and in rhythm with our own being.

Nevertheless, becoming aware of the body's psychological expressivity is not a simple matter. To begin with, in our culture we are more accustomed to pathologizing the body, to sensing its disorders and having them treated without taking into consideration their meaning in the larger context of our own being. This makes it especially difficult for us to re-establish contact with our bodies. It therefore requires a special effort to do so. Often feelings of shame and failure are connected with physical disorders. We expect our bodies to function with a minimum of care and concern, for we want to go on with the business of life. So, we ignore its aches and pains and pursue our work as usual or we consult a doctor who helps us to silence these messages as soon as possible. For certain people, the connection between body and psyche is less evident than for others. I have even known some who cry and wonder why 'this fluid is running from their eyes'.

The woman in the next example had continual messages from her body, but it took a long time for her to realize their importance. She consulted me for quite another reason. But, as I shall show through the detailed description of one of our crucial hours, she came to be aware of her body as an intimate reflection of her true self. At the end of our work, her major physical symptom had practically disappeared, for she had found a new order, more suited to her own life and her needs: she lived more clearly in accord with her own rhythms, as they were expressed in her body and her psyche.

Mrs X consulted me when her daughter began having migraine headaches. The family doctor who examined the girl was able to assure her that nothing was physically wrong. He suggested psychotherapy. One interview with the 10-year-old girl revealed that she felt under extraordinary pressure to do well in school; she thought that this was most important for her mother. The next day I called the mother and asked her to come for an hour in order to discuss the problem.

The woman who arrived at the appointed time, exactly on time, rang the bell timidly and entered with a stiff, yet elegant gait. She was extremely well-dressed, everything matching and in place. She looked beautiful, although somewhat rigid and artificial. During our hour I told her the impression that I had got from the talk with her daughter and asked about the importance of the girl's achievements for her. She spoke then of her own need to be a good enough mother. If her child was happy and healthy and did well socially and at school, she could feel all right about the way she was bringing her up. Further discussion revealed how essential it was for her that the girl 'turn out' well and also why this was so. Mrs X had been married before and divorced; her second marriage *had* to work out: she had to prove to the world, and especially to her concerned parents, that she had done the right thing in leaving her first husband. She was actually, herself, under tremendous pressure to succeed, to make this marriage work. And part of the proof had to be her daughter's good upbringing and achievements.

We are here, once again, in the presence of a very limited and limiting self-image. Mrs X needed to show the world how happy and successful she, her marriage, and her daughter were. This order was evidently too restricted to correspond to the ups and downs she met in life. It left no room for failure, for unhappiness, for conflicts, or for disappointments of any kind. All of that was unacceptable for her; it meant chaos and had to be rejected, ignored, suppressed, repressed.

It is interesting to note, although Mrs X mentioned it *en passant*, that she had been suffering from migraine headaches herself for the past ten years, that is, as she realized on further reflection, since she remarried. But these headaches of hers were only bothersome; she was used to them and generally just went to bed with strong medication when they broke out. She could obviously integrate her own migraines into her self-image. But if her daughter was suffering from the same symptom, then her image of herself as a good enough mother was seriously threatened. That meant chaos for her: it could destroy the world she had worked so hard to build.

Mrs X decided to come to therapy herself, for it had become evident to her through our talk that she herself was under pressure and that she was, without consciously wanting to, transferring this pressure to her daughter. During our work together we came to discover and to understand the kind of order according to which she had been living for the past ten years. We investigated its motivations and its meaning for her. And we came to find its roots in her early years when, as the only child of her divorced mother, she did her best to make Mommy proud of her. In this context her need to prove to her mother and to the world that she was successful, despite a preliminary mismatch, acquired a new dimension of meaning. It showed the extent to which she was identified with her mother, who had also been through a divorce and had managed so well to bring her up.

We came to discover and examine the various times in her life previously when other points of view had expressed themselves in physical and psychological states without, however, ever having reached the critical point. In this light we saw compulsive thoughts of sickness and death which she had had repeatedly as a child, then later depressive states she developed at the time of her first marriage, and finally, the migraine headaches which began when she remarried. She had always managed then to go on, repressing what appeared now as early indications that this order was too static and sterile and unadapted to her own, real needs. But Mrs X first felt as if she were being overwhelmed by chaos when her daughter's migraines erupted. This was the critical point: at this time she realized that she needed to examine her old order. Chaos had erupted into her well-ordered world. She felt definitely destabilized: something was happening within her: she was moved by chaos.

Our work together lasted three years. During this time we devoted ourselves to discovering the order which had marked Mrs X's life until now and we tried to find a more flexible order that was both realistic and individual. We devoted our attention to her present experiences and her feeling reactions to them; we delved into her fantasies, both waking and dreaming; and we called up memories of the past. Also, in time, we could focus on her physical sensations and their meaning.

It was not easy for Mrs X to re-establish contact with her so long neglected inner being. When I asked her how it made her feel, for example, when her husband complained that his shirts were not ironed properly, she did not know at first. It was just normal; it happened all the time; she was used to it. Only slowly and after I had suggested to her that we needed to develop and make use of a kind of 'inner scan' could she imagine what it might mean to pay attention to her emotions. Gradually she became sensitive to what was happening within herself and also in the world around her. She could see that her husband only complained about his shirts when he was especially nervous because of his work and that his nagging made her feel sad. Later on she realized that it also made her angry. But it was a big step to this realization.

It was an even bigger step for her to become aware of her body and its communications. I tried to initiate this awareness during our hours by asking her from time to time not only how it made her feel, for example to be late for a session, but also where she sensed this feeling in her body. At first she was seldom able to locate the tension that she felt. Sometimes I would then ask her how a specific part of her body was feeling or even tell her, for example, that her shoulders seemed particularly high and stiff. In order to illustrate the way in which Mrs X learned to focus on her body and its long neglected needs, I shall describe an hour in which we approached a difficult moment from the point of view of her psyche and her body, establishing a direct contact between the two.

Mrs X arrived for her hour in a rush: she was very busy, had so much to do: fetch her daughter after school, go and pick up her husband, bring the cleaning lady home, go shopping and prepare for a reception at her house that same evening. Such a schedule was not unusual for her, but she felt particularly stressed that day. Because of the intensity of the feelings, I felt it might be useful to get more deeply involved with them, choosing this occasion to 'dilate the moment', to allow it to take up as much room as possible. I asked Mrs X if she could concentrate her entire attention on her stress and try to locate it in her body. As she did so, she found that her chest felt heavy under some weight and that her breathing was constricted. It felt as if a ton of lead were pressing her down. Most uncomfortable was the trouble she was having in breathing freely. She stayed with this sensation which remained in her chest, creating more or fewer breathing problems as she concentrated on it. Then I asked her to try to magnify the sensation, just giving it permission to grow to its maximum in intensity, and while doing so, to pay careful attention to her inner world: to feelings, sensations, images which might then arise. After a while she said that she felt as if a car was rushing toward at her at full speed. It got closer and closer and finally grabbed her up in its path and pushed her along in front of it. And so, she found herself being pushed along by the car travelling at full speed. I asked her to continue to follow the sensation and the image and to see what happened. After a few minutes Mrs X began to cry very quietly. She was able to tell me that the image had suddenly changed: she saw herself as a little girl, picking flowers in her favourite little meadow. The scene was quiet and delightful; she felt peaceful and contented. She was relieved and, at the same time, sad. Such peaceful moments of being alone and just caring for her own quiet pleasures in nature had become rare in her life. Especially since her remarriage she had allowed herself to be propelled by events, to become the doer for everyone else; she had come to neglect herself and her own needs. And she remembered how much she used to enjoy being out of doors, in nature, how much pleasure she used to get from just quietly picking flowers somewhere. And this she had not done in years. Such havens of quiet and care for herself had been sacrificed in favour of her ideal self-image which had no place in it for useless moments of inactivity.

The meadow scene became a 'guiding image' in Mrs X's subsequent life. She recalled it and called upon it whenever she realized that she was concentrating too much on achieving perfection. She tried to grant it space by devoting more time to this other side of her being. The image of herself as a child in the meadow provided an important counterbalance to the perfect woman she otherwise so pushed herself to be. It therefore contributed to expanding Mrs X's self-image: she could also be the child who felt joy and peace in nature and not only the successful housewife and mother.

This hour definitely triggered a developmental leap. All of a sudden Mrs X became capable of putting herself first sometimes. She could take the point of view of her own inner child seriously and tend to it. She no longer lived exclusively in the perfectly ordered world of her ideal self-image. After so many hours in therapy of trying to get in touch with herself again, suddenly she had the impression that she was real. The experience of her child had come very much alive through this dialogue with her emotions, her body, and her imagination.

Mrs X was so impressed by her body's communicativeness in this hour that she began to try out ways of contacting it on her own. When she felt a migraine coming on at home she would retire to her bedroom and work with what she was sensing. Lying on her bed, she would concentrate on her pain, allowing it to lead her to images, memories, associations, feelings. In this way she became aware of the conflicts and her emotional reactions to them that were provoking the headache. On other occasions she could take a step back from the event at hand and, examining it, come to realize what was causing the tension she felt in her head. She then tried to attack the underlying problems in a more direct manner. Frequently she realized that she was just pushing herself too much (like the car of her fantasy) and needed more meadow. Then she would either slow down or go out for a walk. Sometimes she noted that she was containing anger towards her husband or her daughter. Instead of swallowing it, as she was wont, she tried to open up and speak about the problem directly. In this way and in others, Mrs X became able to sense her states, especially the tense ones, with the help of her 'body-seismograph', and to find adaptations that were more adequate, i.e. that were ultimately more satisfying for her.

The session that prodded Mrs X to make this developmental leap took place at the beginning of our third year of work together. She completed therapy at the end of that year. And I can say that she had become 'someone more rounded and complete' (June 1953–79, XII: 84). She no longer held fast to such a rigid order and its restricted self-image, but had become a woman with feelings and desires, with goals and interests that she had not even suspected three years before. She took good care of her daughter, who, by the way, was well. Her migraine headaches had ceased shortly after her mother began therapy, for the pressure on her diminished rapidly.

It is helpful to recall here a point that we made about Mrs X in Chapter 4: her order had become so static that no new order was conceivable before her daughter became the symptom carrier. The girl's migraines helped Mrs X to open up and confront her situation in a way that her previous psychological and physical symptoms had never managed to. The latter had never 'moved' her enough to stimulate the need for growth and transformation. Her critical point was only reached when her daughter was afflicted. This occurrence provoked chaos: Mrs X could not reconcile such a fact with her old order and its perfectionistic self-image.

The new order was definitely more suited to Mrs X's present life: it included different activities, from massage to long walks alone or in the company of her family. It encompassed not only business receptions and social obligations but also a group of friends with whom she felt at home. In brief, we can say that it was personal, as it was oriented to Mrs X herself and was in accord with her own unique and individual being.

This order revolved around and grew out of Mrs X's learning to sense what went on within herself and in her world As she became willing and able to reflect on her life experiences directly, she also became able to sort them out, to understand and accept them within the broader context of her being.

The inclusion of the physical sensations one feels along with the emotional reactions one experiences and the attention paid to one's images, imagination, fantasies, and dreams all go into making the psychotherapeutic situation one of chaos initiation. We develop means of dealing with chaos through encouraging repeated encounters with it. The confusion caused by the initial experience is met and then retreats into the background as the person becomes increasingly capable of entering into direct contact with their own emotional experiences. Thus, the retreat from reality can be reversed and, at the same time, the person comes to discover many new facets of their being. Previously unknown and even unacceptable traits assemble into a new coherency which can encompass divergencies, irregularities, disorder, in short, chaos itself.

VARIATIONS ON THE THEME OF CHAOS AND ORDER

The therapeutic approach to chaos is determined by the specific needs of each individual who seeks help. In the above-mentioned cases, the step from the chaotic initial experience to the search for a more organic order was relatively smooth and natural. In the following cases it was not.

Some people who are faced with chaos are not capable of engaging in the encounter. Their experience is an extreme emergency; they panic and try to swim back towards dry land as soon as possible. And all they want afterwards is to stay as far away from the water as possible.

I am thinking here of a man who, eaten up by jealousy, had a terrifying panic attack on the way to work one morning. He did not, however, realize that it was his jealousy which prompted this extreme reaction. All he sensed was the panic, the fear that he could not go on, that he would fall down in the middle of the street. The few months during which he came to therapy once a week were devoted to helping him to digest the frightening experience and to retrieve his self-confidence. We managed to find out what had triggered the attack: he had suddenly developed fantasies that his wife was cheating on him with his best friend. From what he told of himself and his life, it became apparent that his fears of losing his wife stemmed from deep-seated insecurities. He had lived with them all of his life: they were related to the fact that his mother had left him when he was a small child. But, for the man himself, these interrelations were not evident. Trying to prompt him to look at the past, his former life and his unresolved feelings of abandonment continually led to a dead-end. He could not, at that time at least, turn his glance inward. He fixated rather on his wife and her eventual infidelity.

It was not possible to go on to discover the deeper, underlying patterns which determined chaos, nor to find another order in which separation and insecurity could take their place within the context of life. The man's most urgent need was to recover from the fear that had so unexpectedly come over him. And so, after our ten sessions together, when he felt sufficiently re-established in his old order, he left. Perhaps some day he will come back. I hope so, for subsequent destabilizations are bound to occur in the future when he is faced with uncertainties in his life. Perhaps then he will find the energy and interest to pursue his exploration of his inner world.

Some people who consult a therapist in a chaotic crisis may at that time hesitate to pursue any further chaos encounters in the framework of therapy. Later on, however, they can develop the desire and need to do so. George was one such person. He had come because of a disappointment with his girlfriend. After he managed to get through the difficult depression which had overcome him, he decided that he would like to go on to discover why he had reacted in that way, what his depression had to do with him as a person, what it might have to do with his own particular patterns of relating to people.

In therapy we also meet people for whom chaos is especially threatening because they actually possess limited capacities for dealing with it. Of central importance in these cases is helping the person achieve a kind of peace again after what has been for them a wracking storm. Perhaps we can help them to find a little bit larger piece of dry land on which to stand. That is, we try to increase consciousness as much as possible. We work at discerning the precipitating event. We see chaos as the end of a chain of actions and reactions – a natural reaction, for example, to a deception in love, loss of a partner, marital conflicts, or a trying situation at work. The therapy can then be drawn to a close, for no further insights are possible. In the future, the person may (hopefully) become more readily aware of the preliminary signs of chaos's eruption. Other cases do, however, exist which cannot draw further profit from the work accomplished: they repeatedly fall into the same types of difficulties without realizing it. The basic problem is an insufficiency in the capacity for self-reflection.

I would like to present here the case of Sabena, a 22-year-old kindergarten teacher. She was suffering from the most varied physical symptoms – from repeated bouts of colds and flu to palpitations and stomach aches. Whenever she felt her body in a state of disorder, she was convinced that her death could not be far off. These physical symptoms automatically triggered chaos in her. Sabena had already been through several operations when I met her. And she had become accustomed to taking pain-killers and tranquillizers. Furthermore, she was used to drinking large quantities of alcohol – to calm her nerves on the most varied occasions: when she felt unhappy, when she felt nervous after work, when her fantasies of impending doom and death became unbearable for her. Sabena's main need was finding some calm in this stormy inner life: she was not interested in further trying to comprehend her body symptoms as an element of her sensitivity; she did not want to consult her dreams and was even rather hesitant about discussing problems that turned up in her life. What she wanted was to be calmed, to be tranquillized, to be reassured that everything was all right. That had brought her to consult many medical people and to undergo many diverse treatments.

A dream which she reported one day shows what one must surmise from Sabena's attitude towards therapy: she was not able to get involved with chaos, for her fear was too great. She dreamed that the dam in her village broke and that there was a huge flood. The apartment she lived in with her mother was turned topsy-turvy. Suddenly she saw her little brother buoyed up in the water in a flimsy toy boat. She awoke, frightened. Evidently, Sabena's capacity for dealing with the chaotic waters was scarcely sufficient: the life-boat is too flimsy. Like the cockle-shell life-boats of Edith and Snow White, it is too fragile for the violent floods. The threat posed by the uncontrolled waters can be understood as a reflection of Sabena's imagination of chaos: violent, dangerous, frightening. She did not feel well enough equipped to confront chaos, but rather needed to be reassured that everything was going to be all right. Her background helps us to understand this attitude: both her mother and her grandmother had taken tranquillizers and drunk alcohol to calm themselves all their adult lives. Sabena had seen this means of dealing with chaos – avoiding it; she had learned from these models and could not, for the moment at least, imagine any other possible ways of dealing with chaos. She feared any direct confrontation with such overwehlming forces: they seemed too threatening for her.

Actually, what became apparent for me during the year we worked together was that Sabena was an extremely sensitive and unconscious person: she lived according to the butterfly principle and was repeatedly gravely destabilized by events. Her sensitivity was potentially a positive trait: had she been able to sense her unstable moments and reflect on them and what caused them, she would have been able to distinguish the elements of chaos and find appropriate ways of meeting it. But, as we have seen, this was not possible. The patterns of avoidance which she had learned at home early on taught her to treat the signals of her 'body seismograph' in a repressive manner. She had never learned to pay attention to or to reflect on them. Her tools for chaos encounter were, in consequence, sadly undeveloped.

After our year together, therefore, Sabena had not come to find a more personal order: she had not become more flexible, but she had come to realize that her body signals were potentially valuable. She went to see her family doctor less frequently and began to practise sports as a way of letting off the pent-up steam she had in her: she had discovered that she was sensitive and that she retained anger and many other emotional reactions. But she could not find other more adequate ways of dealing with her inner life. She still felt that her sensitivity was rather a disadvantage in her life. And, although she did manage to find other ways of granting it expression, she continued to drink and to take tranquillizers whenever she felt particularly upset and nervous.

The therapeutic chaos encounter can consist of a combination of medication and talk: allowing the person to talk of the crisis and of how difficult it is for him. It can be expanded to an attempt to understand the crisis and the fact that it must have something important to say within the context of the individual's life. And it can go on from here to become a search for organic order, an order that involves a broader, more flexible, and more tolerant self-image. How far each therapy goes on depends on individuals and their own specific needs and wishes.

As long as the patterns of chaos avoidance – be they extreme ordering systems (compulsions and obsessions like touch and wash rituals, anorexic eating and vomiting, etc.) or escape into drugs or drug-like diversions (flight into fantasy worlds or over-activity, etc.) – still function satisfactorily, the person feels no need to discover and develop means of confrontation. Only when these defences break down is one faced with the formlessness of the chaotic abyss. Only when a chink in the fortification appears does the re-examination of the situation emerge as an important alternative. In this connection it is important to recall what we observed in the schizophrenic's timetable: the closer the eruption of chaos, the more extreme the compensatory order or escape. Paradoxically, at the peak of order, chaos often breaks in.

Frequently anorexics, depressive people, people living with strict compulsions and obsessions, do not themselves sense chaos; nor do they seek help. Living within their system, they have managed to retreat from chaos so successfully that they actually do not experience it themselves. In such cases, their milieu often reacts. This dimension of their reality comes to the fore as a concerned friend or relative, sensing that something is wrong, suggests therapy. This was the case with Anne, who has been described in this chapter. Therapeutically speaking, such an entrance into therapy is difficult. Such persons do not feel the threat of chaos themselves. As long as they live closed off in their system they remain well-defended. Their critical point has not been reached: they have not felt the necessity of finding a more suitable order. Thus far only their milieu has become alarmed. Such people's bodies and psyches have not yet begun to sense the need for readaptation. According to our scientific model, this must mean that transformation and the readiness for it are, as yet, a long way off.

Before concluding this review of the therapy of chaos, I must mention one specific type of client who is, however, in my experience, rare in therapy. Such clients do not seek help because of an unsettling chaos experience and often have no specific complaints. Perhaps they are dissatisfied with themselves and their development, or have the feeling that they could make more out of themselves and their lives. But their dissatisfaction is not so bothering as to reach the critical point that makes transformation possible.

These people successfully manage to avoid chaos by maintaining an extreme distance from reality as well as by their chameleon-like shifting from one point of view to the other. Often they focus on the outside world where they perceive inimical forces of order which they oppose. Instead of identifying with a rigid and restricting order, they project just such order onto the surrounding world. Much of their lives' energies are devoted to fighting it; it is as if they were shadow-boxing with order so as to avoid facing their unconscious need for order and orientation and their equally unconscious fears of chaos.

Thus the difference between them and those of whom we have mainly spoken until now is not as great as it may have seemed at first. Here, too, the work entails developing the tools with which to confront chaos and stimulating the search for organic order. Here too, we need to retrieve the natural flexibility of the point of view, renewing, or even developing for the first time, the capacity to focus on the inner world. In this work especially the body takes on a supreme importance, for it is here that these people can get in touch with emotions and sensations that they can recognize as their own. Finding a grounding for their inklings, their timid efforts at registering and expressing feelings in their own physicality helps them to differentiate between what belongs to them and what does not.

Charlie was one such person. He came because his girlfriend said that therapy would be good for him. He did not know why she thought so or what she meant by that remark. But he figured that he could try it: it would be a new experience and, who knows, maybe it would be good. Charlie had the feeling that he might be able to make more out of himself and his life; maybe this was one way to do so.

With time it became apparent that Charlie lived cut off from his inner world and spent his energies (1) in trying to avoid encountering it and (2) fighting order wherever he saw it. These two points were related. Charlie was apparently afraid of being nailed down, of being cornered and forced to face his own inner reality. And it was his avoidance of 'being nailed down' that actually characterized him. He accordingly feared and fought anything that smelled like order, anyone who might represent order. For him it meant the compulsion to conform; and that he would not and could not do: it was like being caught in a trap. Charlie had managed to live most of his life through opposing order in the outside world. Whenever he was confronted by an authority figure, he flew up in a rage of protest. And so, he had had severe problems at school, where he ridiculed his teachers and made himself feared and disliked. His school work suffered as a result: why should he work for this or that test, the teacher was an idiot anyway? When he finally managed to finish school and get a job, he frequently flared up at his boss. So, he changed jobs rather often. But his authority complex and the fear of conforming to order made him fall into other loaded situations: he had fights with bus drivers, with policemen, with restaurant managers. The ugly face of order was ever-present and had to be attacked again and again. His reactions then were extreme and unpredictable; what for someone else may have seemed a slight matter, was for him a criminal case in which he had to fight back. Here we see once again the butterfly principle at work. The instability is determined by the virulent authority complex which was unconscious.

With this type of oppositional attitude, he had managed very well thus far. And this is probably why people like Charlie generally do not seek therapy: they can live relatively well in society and feel all right about themselves because they see the enemy outside and fight him there: they can thus act out opposition to order in conflict with authorities (from police to political parties, from parents to bosses) and deny their own, human need for order and orientation. Charlie was lacking in orientation: with no points of view he could call his own, he was buffeted about like a piece of driftwood. Whereas his own very human need for order was denied: instead, order was demonized and projected onto the world around him.

The therapeutic situation was understandably difficult for Charlie. He sensed in me a representative of the forces of order which, in a way, I was. For I was concerned with trying to help him discover who he was, what was going on inside him, what his points of view were, and what they meant to him. He saw me as a strict and judgemental policeman. At times he stressed my punitive manner, at others I was a sibylline oracle, making pronouncements which he felt were important. He sought and fought truth and direction in me.

Naturally, under such circumstances it was impossible to establish a fruitful therapeutic alliance. We could not work together to help Charlie discover his inner world, but were like two opponents, each on his own side of the fence. Charlie had the impression that I was after him and I had the impression that he was running away from himself and from me. Forming and maintaining a relationship with me was inconceivable for him: it was a trap that he had to avoid falling into.

Needless to say, hours with Charlie were a dizzy matter. Sometimes I felt as if I were being rocked in a boat on stormy seas. For Charlie maintained a kaleidoscopic distance from me and from himself. He spoke in a detached fashion about people and life, generalizing, intellectualizing, forming hypotheses, and making interpretations of what he saw going on in the surrounding world. He reflected on people, on life, and made sure all the while that he did not get emotionally involved himself. Everything was possible from his distanced perspective. He was nowhere and everywhere. My efforts to find out what he was actually trying to say, or where he was, and what all of this meant for him were repeated failures. Interventions aimed at such clarifications just sent Charlie running off in some other direction.

I remember one particular hour in which this kaleidoscopic distance became especially apparent as a defence against chaos. He was talking about a woman he had met and described the way she had avoided looking at him. He went on and on to suggest why she had done so, what women were like, how the battle of the sexes was culturally determined. It suddenly occurred to me that, judging from what he had said about her, the woman might have interested him. When I inquired what she was like, he described a very attractive, sporty young woman; and he spoke in an animated fashion. However, when I inquired about his feelings for her he began again to talk of the most varied things – of parties and fashion models, of sports and his other interests. After listening for five minutes to this 'paraphernalia', I asked him point blank if he might not be attracted to her. He was taken aback, became quiet, and finally assented. And from there he went on to spread before me kaleidoscopic images of love and life.

In this interchange it became all too clear that Charlie was running away from his inner world, from feeling it, examining it, taking it seriously, and acting accordingly. He feared to turn his glance inward and so he put up a smoke-screen between himself and his emotions.

These observations provided essential diagnostic indications. They revealed the extent to which Charlie was cut off from himself and showed the way in which we had to continue. First of all, it was essential to be able to discuss the distance Charlie put between himself and the world and his tendency to avoid contact with himself and with me. We had to become partners in trying to understand this automatic mechanism that was getting in the way of any real communication. It became important for Charlie to contact the ground under his feet, to find an anchor in reality, and a tangible connection to himself and his own feelings. Like all of the other people described so far, Charlie, too, needed most of all to become sensitive to himself and his emotional life, to come to discover the various points of view that dwelt in him, and, finally, to find a sense of order that corresponded to his needs, an order that would be supportive of his life, and no longer merely an inimical force which he needed to constellate and then to fight. His archetypal human need for order needed to be satisfied in a way that was suitable for him.

As in our previous examples, the work was devoted to developing Charlie's sensitivity; that meant allowing himself to contact and to be moved by what he experienced, permitting himself to feel the various things that went on within him, and to accept them instead of pushing them away. We needed to take his feelings, his dreams, his fantasies seriously and to consider whatever they seemed to be expressing as inherently valuable points of view which had to be integrated within Charlie's image of himself. In this connection, work with Charlie's physical sensations became very important. Finding palpable proof of his own, personal being in his body ultimately enabled Charlie to indentify with what he was saying, to recognize emotions, and to call them his own. He could no longer deny them or run away from them, for he felt them in his own body.

A critical point in our work was marked by the session I am about to describe here. Charlie came in and began to talk about his boss, about management techniques about business and economy. He was up in the clouds. Also perceptible, however, was a tinge of irritation. I became intent upon helping Charlie to sense and express this feeling. And so I interrupted his elaborations and asked how he was feeling at the moment. After preliminary denials of feeling anything special, he began to apply himself to discovering what was going on within.

After a while he found that he was a bit nervous, excited, but could not define the kind of agitation he was feeling. I asked him to try to find the place in his body where the sensation was the most intense. His stomach immediately became the centre of energy from which loud signals were being sent out. After quite some time of concentrating his attention on his stomach and what it might be trying to express, Charlie began perceiving various emotions. He felt pressure there, coming from his boss, but also from his own incapacities; then disappointment surfaced, disappointment with himself which, it seemed to him, the boss also felt towards him. Then, beside his boss appeared his father. And the disappointment became deeper, more destructive. Frustration with the lack of support he had had from his father led to slight feelings of anger towards him. But this anger was buried very deep and Charlie could hardly imagine it, let alone formulate it. Towards the end of our hour, a deep sadness arose, sadness that he had never felt the strong, helping hand of a father in his life, sadness that he had had to act out his frustration with his unsupportive, yet somehow threatening father in conflicts with authority (or father) figures that he met in the course of the years. He had had a very difficult time with this projection of his father complex onto the outside world: his advancement at school and at work had suffered as a result.

The range of emotions which Charlie had managed to contact and express told us a great deal about him and this central problem of his development. Reflecting on this hour in subsequent sessions brought back many long-forgotten memories. We were able to reconstruct what must have happened to him early on. Charlie had had an emotionally absent father. From his perspective, as a little boy, father was big and threatening, for he was generally silent and did not participate in the boy's life. Charlie consequently became afraid of him, yet he also needed and sought him. The only way he could reach this silent giant was by creating problems. He did not dare to do so at home, but at school, for example, he made such a nuisance of himself that reports of his behaviour reached home. That is, his father, informed about his pranks and impossibly argumentative ways, would become angry and discipline him. But this was a form of attention that Charlie managed to get from his father. His behaviour was determined by this deeply unconscious motivation: getting his father to devote time and energy to him.

As he grew, Charlie's behaviour continued automatically as it had been in these early years. He would still now, as an adult, provoke aggressive show downs with authority figures. He was still somehow hoping to gain the attention of a father in this way. His deepest desires were that this father would support him. But, with this oppositional behaviour, Charlie lived in emotional seclusion. He felt extremely insecure, for lacking in the necessary paternal encouragement, he had never acquired any self-assurance. He felt worthless, and so he withdrew from contact with himself and with the outside world.

Evidently such an adaptive pattern, the result of an unfortunately empty relationship with his father, was unsuitable for Charlie as an adult. It did not help him to get the support he sought and it also got in the way of his finding appropriate ways of being in his present, real life situation. It also prevented him from finding an orientation in himself.

It was time to seek a new order which could stimulate Charlie's development. A fruitful relationship with inner ordering principles was necessary. But this meant that Charlie had to find means of contacting his inner life. As I mentioned above, an introspective attitude was very difficult for him to achieve. But, as we see in the hour described here, the contact with his body and what he felt there provided Charlie with a reliable instrument for testing what belonged to himself and what did not.

When Charlie finished his six years of therapy (it had taken this length of time, for Charlie had really had a long way to go) he was pleased. He had come to discover potentialities within himself that he had actually felt, but hardly dared hope to develop before. He felt more secure in himself, for his foundations were broader and firmer than ever. He gained the courage to confront his own father directly and, in several long conversations, found out that the latter really had been emotionally absent in his youth, for he was very unhappy with Charlie's mother but did not dare to leave her. He did not know what to do, so he just stayed and withdrew emotionally. As a result, the boy got the impression that his father did not appreciate him but, in fact, his father just did not see him. He was too preoccupied with himself and his inner retreat from the unpleasant circumstances to have any energy left for the boy. An absent father can be as harmful as an authoritarian one. And parents unhappy in their marriage can be as destructive as those who reject or mistreat their children.

Through his lengthy and intensive work in therapy, Charlie was able to develop an inner paternal image from which he drew support and encouragement. He became a realistic young man whose path was grounded in his own being. Oriented to himself, he no longer needed to seek and fight authority figures in the world outside.

In this final chapter we have taken a close look at psychotherapeutic chaos encounter and the concomitant search for organic order. In terms of the aquatic initiation rites of Chapter 2, we are aiming at a renewal of the personality through direct contact with the chaotic forces – be they water, emotional states, or other unconscious material. We have spoken here mainly in terms of our scientific model: of discerning patterns in chaos and allowing for the emergence of new order out of chaos (by entering into communication with the diverse aspects of one's being).

But neither in the realm of nature, nor in that of humanity, can order be achieved once and for all. The Babylonians, but also the Polynesians, showed us that. In the course of our lives we are continually confronted with new and challenging situations which can provoke chaos in us. Adequate means of encounter cannot be found and maintained throughout a lifetime. Despite all of what we have said in the foregoing about the constant readaptations that

belong to life, it must be stressed here that such readaptations are
no easy matter for us. Unlike natural organisms, we seem to tend
to varying degrees of stasis: once we have found an order that suits
us, we become accustomed to it and cannot so easily abandon it.
It has worked in the past; why should it not continue to work
now? The old order is comfortable, has the ease of habit to its
advantage. And the instinct to establish habits, to settle down into
the known and comfortable, to seek warmth and security in the
known, characterizes us as human beings.

Thus, each and every time we apply ourselves to confronting a
new situation in an appropriate manner we are going against this
instinct, just as, in distinguishing the elements of chaos, we are
performing an *opus contra naturam*: we are swimming upstream.
Dividing the waters of chaos and controlling them is not a natural
capacity of man in the face of nature. Furthermore, lest we become
possessed by the optimistic and heroic images we have described
here, it is important to add that the avoidance patterns we have
seen in the preceding pages, the automatisms of our unexamined
behaviour patterns are very much part of what it means to be
human. This may come as a surprise to us, for we like to believe that
we are eminently conscious, critical and rational beings, prepared
and equipped to 'master' life and its problems. The exclusiveness
of such an image is an illusion: we do not naturally tend to be
Mardukian, nor to adapt spontaneously in the appropriate manner,
evolving naturally from one phase of order to the next.

Such processes are connected with enormous difficulties and
natural resistances. And they must be respected as such, for the
anti-hero is the essential counterpart to the hero that we like to
imagine that we are. Wanting to run away and hide from the
unknown is a spontaneous, instinctive reaction. What counts in
the long run is not that we stand and face the monster, but that
we realize and can admit to ourselves that we are afraid and would
like to flee. In that moment we accept our weaknesses and, at
the same time, our own inner child, its doubts, anxieties, and
insecurities. This very real, but long neglected aspect of ourselves
has managed to get our attention. What we have been referring to
as chaos encounter can be considered in this light as re-establishing
a relationship with the child in us, reaching out to understand and
comfort it in the face of the darkness and confusion, the suffering
which also belong to life.

Bibliography

Asper, Kathrin (1987) *Verlassenheit und Selbstentfremdung: neue Zugänge zum therapeutischen Verständnis*, Olten und Freiburg im Breisgau, Walter Verlag.

Breuer, R. (1985) 'Das Chaos', *Geo* 7 (24 July)

Brun, Ernst (1985) 'Von Ordnung und Chaos in der Synergetik', *Physik und Didaktik* 4: 289–305 (Munich, Bayerischer Schulbuch Verlag).

Brun, Ernst (1986) 'Ordnung-Hierarchien', in *Neujahrsblatt Naturforschende Gesellschaft*, Zürich, Orell Füssli.

Eliade, Mircea (1975) *Le Sacré et le profane* (*The sacred and the profane*) Paris, Gallimard (originally published as *Das Heilige und das Profane*, Rowohlt, Hamburg, 1957).

Eliade, Mircea (ed.) (1977) *Die Schöpfungsmythen: Aegypter, Sumerer, Hurriter, Hethiter, Kanaaniter und Israeliter* (introduction by M. Eliade), Darmstadt, Wissenschaftliche Buchgesellschaft (first published as *La Naissance du monde*, Paris, Editions du Seuil, 1959).

Frazer, Sir James George (1983) *The Golden Bough: A Study in Magic and Religion* (abridged edition; first published 1922), London, Macmillan.

Gross, Rudolf (1991) 'Chaos und Ordnung: Dynamische Systeme in der Medizin', *Deutsches Arateblatt* 88 (25–6) (24 June): 75–83.

Haken, Hermann (1978) *Synergetics: An Introduction – Non-equilibrium Phase Transitions and Self-organization in Physics, Chemistry and Biology*, 2nd edn, Berlin, Heidelberg, New York, Sprenger.

Haken, Hermann (1986) *Erfolgsgeheimnisse der Natur. Synergetik: Die Lehre vom Zusammenwirken*, Stuttgart, Deutsche Verlagsanstait.

Heidel, Alexander (1974) *The Babylonian Genesis: The Story of Creation*, 2nd edn, Chicago, University of Chicago Press (first published 1942).

Highsmith, Patricia (1980) *Edith's Diary*, Hamondsworth, Penguin Books (first published by Heinemann, 1977).

Jacoby, Mario (1985) *The Longing for Paradise*, Boston, Sigo Press (first published as *Sehnsucht nach dem Paradies*, Fellbach, Verlag Adolf Bonz, 1980).

Jung, Carl Gustav (1953–79) *The Collected Works*, trans. by R.F. Hull, ed. William McGuire, Herbert Read, Michael Fordham, Bollingen Series XX, New York, Pantheon Books; later London and New York, Routledge.

Lehmann, Heinz E. (1980) 'Schizophrenia: a clinical picture', in Freedman, Kaplan, Sedcock and Peters *Comprehensive Textbook of Psychiatry*, London, Williams & Wilkins.

Marjasch, Sonja (1961) 'Vom Ich im Traum', Unpublished paper given to the annual meeting of the Swiss Society for Analytical Psychology in Berne. 9 July 1961

Meyer, Piet (1981) *Kunst und Religion der Lobi*, Zürich, Rietberg Museum.

Ott, Jörg A. Wagner, Günter P. and Wuketits, Franz M. (eds) (1985) *Evolution, Ordnung und Erkenntnis*, Berlin and Hamburg, Paul Parey.

Prigogine, Ilya and Stengers, Isabelle (1984) *Order out of Chaos: Man's New Dialogue with Nature*, Toronto and New York, Bantam Books (first published as *La Nouvelle Alliance*, 1979).

Taylor, Gordon Rattray (1983) *Das Geheimnis der Evolution* (The Great Evolution Mystery), Frankfurt am Main, S. Fischer.

Turgenev, Ivan (1966) *Fathers and Sons*, New York, W.W. Norton (first published in Moscow, 1862).

Weiss, Paul A. (1973) *The Science of Life: The Living System – A System for Living*, New York, Futura.

Further reading on chaos

Becker, Karl, Dörfler, Heinz and Dörfler, Michael (1986) *Computer-graphische Experimente mit Pascal: Ordnung und Chaos in dynamischen Systemen*, Braunschweig/Wiesbaden, Friedrich Vierweg und Sohn.

Breuer, R. (1985) 'Das Chaos', *Geo* no. 7, 24 July.

Brun, E. (1985) 'Von Ordnung und Chaos in der Synergetik', *Physik und Didaktik* 4: 289–306 (Munich, Bayrischer Schulbuch-Verlag).

Brun, E. (1986) 'Ordnung-Hierarchien', in *Neujahrsblatt of the Natur-forschende Gesellschaft in Zürich for 1986*, Zurich, Orell Füssli.

Brun, E., Derighetti, B., Meier, D., Holzner, R. and Ravani, M. (1985) 'Observation of order and chaos in a nuclear spin-flip laser', *Journal of the Optical Society of America*, B/2, no.1, Jan 156–67.

Brun, E., Derighetti, B., Ravani, M. and Meier, P. F. (1985) 'Order and chaos in non-linear NMR: Synergetics at work', unpublished paper for Proceedings of the 7th Specialized Ampère Colloquium, Bucharest, 9–13 September.

Decker, U. and Thomas, H. (1983) 'Unberechenbares Spiel der Natur – die Chaos Theorie', *Bild der Wissensschaft*, 1.

Der Schweizer Buchhandel 5 (1989), 'Der Biologe und die Umweltphilosophin', March.

Forschungsgruppe Komplexe Dynamik, Universität von Bremen: *Harmonie im Chaos: Bilder aus der Theorie der dynamischen Systeme*, 1984; *Schönheit im Chaos: Bilder aus der Theorie komplexer Systeme*, 1985.

Gassmann, Fritz (1990) 'Chaos und Ordnung – Triebfeder der Evolution', *Neue Zürcher Zeitung* no. 265 (14 Nov.), p. 267.

Geo Wissen 2 (1990) 'Chaos und Kreativität', 7 May.

Gleick, James (1987) *Chaos: Making a New Science*, New York, Simon & Schuster.

Meigniez, Robert (1983) *Civitas, ou la Psychanalyse du Chaos*, Paris, Editions Delaru.

Müri, Peter (1986) *Chaos Management*, Egg, Kreativ-Verlag.

Odenwald, Michael (1989) 'Chaos regiert die Welt', *Chancen: Technik und Wissenschaft*, March, pp. 32–7.

Ordre et Désordre; textes des conférences et des entretiens organisés par les 29ièmes Rencontres internationales de Genève, 1983, Neuchâtel, La Baconnière, 1984.

Prigogine, Ilya and Stengers, Isabelle (1984) *Order out Of Chaos: Man's New Dialogue with Nature*, Toronto and New York, Bantam Books.

Rose, W. (1985) 'Die Entdeckung des Chaos', *Die Zeit* no. 3, 11 Jan.

Saperstein, A. M. (1985) 'Chaos: A model for the outbreak of war', *Nature*, 24 May.

Schnabel, Ulrich (1988) 'Ordnung und Chaos', *Die Zeit* no. 41, 7 Oct.

Schütze, Christian (1988) 'Alles ist wie abgerissen', *Suddeutsche Zeitung* 26 Sept.

Schütze, Christian (1988) 'Chaos und Ordnung im Wechselspiel', *Suddeutsche Zeitung* 27 Sept.

Seifritz, W. (1987) 'Was ist ein Gleichgewicht?', *Neue Zürcher Zeitung* no. 208, 9 Sept., p. 95.

Wieland-Burston, Joanne (1989), 'Chaos: ein neuer Weg zur Ordnung?', *Psychologie Heute*, 3 (March): 56–61.

Wieland-Burston, Joanne (1989) 'Ordnungsuche der Seele: chaotische Gefühle', *Schweiz. Handelseitung* no. 31 (3 Aug.), p. 33.

Wieland-Burston, Joanne (1990) 'Chaos in der Seele: wie weiter?', *Leben und Glauben* no. 8 (23 Feb.), pp. 34–7.

Name index

Asper, Kathrin 93

Blake, William 30–1
Breuer, R. 70, 78
Brun, Ernst, 73–4, 75, 77

Claudel, Paul 109, 112

Darwin, Charles 78
Dietrich, Marlene 35
Duchamp Marcel 16

Eldredge, Miles 77–8
Eliade, Mircea 4, 33, 44

Faulkner, William 104
Franz, Ferdinand 92
Frazer, James 42–3

Gould, Stephen 77–8

Haken, Hermann 74
Heidel, Alexander 27–33
Hicks, Edward 67, 68
Highsmith, Patricia 5, 47–53

Jacoby, Mario 103
Joyce, James 104
Jung, Carl Justav 7, 102–3,
  109, 124

Lorenz, Edward N. 78

Marjasch, Sonja 113, 115

Meyer, Piet 36

Picasso, Pablo 103, 104
Plato 20
Poincaré, Henri 70
Prigogine, Ilya 73, 74, 76, 77, 78

Sakharov, André 78
Stengers, Isabelle 74, 76, 78

Taylor, Gordon Rattray 77, 79
Turgenev, Ivan 4–5, 53, 56–60

von Sternberg, Joseph 35

Weiss, Paul 79, 100, 101-2

Subject index